Learning to Dance with

Life

A Guide for
High Achieving Women

PAMELA THOMPSON

LEARNING TO DANCE WITH LIFE
A Guide for High Achieving Women

Copyright © 2015 PAMELA THOMPSON

Published by:
Transformation Books
211 Pauline Drive #513
York, PA 17402
www.TransformationBooks.com

ISBN: 978-0-9862901-3-8
Library of Congress Control Number: 2015943767

Cover Design by: Ranilo Cabo
Editor: Ellen Turnbull

Printed in the United States of America

A portion of the proceeds from the sale of this book will be donated to charities the author supports.

Dedication

To Mom, who inspired me in her
gentle and loving way, and from
whom I learned so much.

Praise for *Learning to Dance with Life*

"In this timely and engaging book, Pam Thompson shares her powerful message of how you can be successful in business, and at the same time, be happy, healthy and grounded. This book provides practical tools and proven strategies to help you cultivate improved health, happiness, clarity and fulfillment in your life. If you want to thrive in business and in life, read this book!"

Christine Comaford, Neuroscience-Based Leadership Coach at SmartTribes Institute and NY Times Bestselling Author of *SmartTribes* and *Rules for Renegades*
http://smarttribesinstitute.com/

"As a high-achieving woman, graduating with honors from Harvard Law School, I found my greatest success when I left 'the treadmill' and began to listen to my inner voice and do the work I really came to do, inspired work. I'm so delighted that Pam Thompson is helping other achievers focus on their greatest achievement—finding peace and purpose. You're so worth this life of joy and peace!"

Tama Kieves, USA Today featured visionary career catalyst and best-selling author of This Time I Dance! Creating the Work you Love, A Year Without Fear: 365 Days of Magnificence, and Inspired & Unstoppable
www.TamaKieves.com

"If you're tired of living life "on a treadmill" and want to get off, Learning to Dance with Life: A Guide for High Achieving Women *is a must read. Pam Thompson provides answers to the question of how to stay healthy, happy, and grounded while living your passion, and engages you with proven tools and strategies. A valuable resource for women in business."*

Sage Lavine, CEO of Conscious Women Entrepreneurs, Host of the International Women on Purpose summits

www.sagelavine.com

"Insightful, inspiring, and engaging. In *Learning to Dance with Life: A Guide for High Achieving Women,* Pam shares proven strategies to support you in experiencing more fun, fulfillment, clarity, energy, and success in life and business. All this, while making a positive difference in the world!"

Debra L. Reble, Ph.D. author of the award-winning book *Soul-Hearted Partnership: Creating the Ultimate Experience of Love, Passion, and Intimacy*

www.debrareble.com

Acknowledgments

To Dad who has always encouraged me to be the best I can be, and who inspired me to believe that anything is possible.

To my loving partner, Alan, for his unwavering support. Thanks for enabling me to soar, feeding my love of adventure, and making me laugh.

To all those busy women, who took the time to be interviewed and shared their precious stories, and to my amazing clients from whom I've learned so much.

To my thoughtful and skilled editor, Ellen Turnbull, who did such a great job of editing this, my first book.

To Christine Kloser and her team at Transformation Books who supported me every step of the way and made it possible to birth this book.

Contents

PART III:
Sharing Your Dance with the World

Introduction

For many years my life was all about work. I worked long hours, went to bed thinking about work, and often awoke with work on my mind. In the morning I would hit the ground running, rather than take time to ground myself and quiet my busy mind. During interactions with others, I was often thinking of the next thing on my to-do list, rather than being totally present with the conversation. I was like a spinning top; always *doing* and rarely *being*.

I typically took work home on weekends when I worked for someone else and worked night and day when I started my own consulting and coaching businesses. I would check one project off the list and immediately get on with the next one, rarely taking time to bask in the joy of my accomplishments.

Reflecting on those days, becoming a mother of two children was likely my saving grace. They "made me" take time off on weekends and some evenings to spend quality time with them. If I hadn't had kids, who knows what a crazy person I might have become! My kids helped me to understand unconditional love and to experience the fun and fulfillment associated with being fully present while with them.

At this phase in my life, I'm called to reach out to and support driven women who have made work a priority over their own health, their relationships, and their well-being. Living life as a High Achieving Woman can take an unhealthy toll on your body, mind and relationships at home and at work unless there is balance. I know this from personal experience.

Learning to Dance with Life: A Guide for High Achieving Women provides proven strategies and powerful practices to support you to create more balance in your life and to experience more clarity, focus and fulfillment. It provides you with answers to the question of how to stay healthy, happy, and grounded while living your passion.

I've based the strategies and practices offered in this book on my own research and experiences as a coach, mentor and consultant within diverse cultures around the world. They are supported by evidence from neuroscience and Eastern psychology. I also draw on the positive evidence of the health-promoting and healing benefits of the arts.

The book is divided into three sections. Part I identifies a number of attributes of High Achieving Women and explores the impact the negative attributes have on us. The attributes are based on my own experience and work with clients, and have been confirmed by in-depth interviews with 20 High Achieving Women from North America, the United Kingdom, and Asia. Part I also sets you up for your journey from living life on a treadmill to "dancing with life." It supports you as you explore change and your response to change, and provides practical tips for overcoming resistance and moving forward.

Part II introduces the concept of what I call *Creative Living;* a conscious journey that cultivates improved health, happiness, fulfillment and inner peace in your life. This section outlines the seven elements of *Creative Living* and provides seven keys to integrating them into your life.

Exercises are woven throughout the chapters so you can actively engage in learning and integrating the keys to *Creative Living* into your life. A complimentary workbook is available for download at *www.creativelivingcommunity.com/workbook/*

Part III is about sharing your dance with the world. It focuses on ways to share and continue your learning and provides opportunities to get involved in the *Creative Living* Community. It ends with a vision of what the world can be like when we dance with life.

Why am I writing this book?

> I'm called to get the message out about the negative impacts on our bodies, minds, and relationships that result from driving ourselves, not listening to our bodies, and living in our left brain.

Over the past 10 to 15 years, many of my ambitious friends and colleagues have been diagnosed with cancer, auto-immune disorders (such as fibromyalgia), burnout, and adrenal fatigue, and I believe an unbalanced lifestyle was a contributing factor. I have been close to burnout several times myself. I know what it feels like to be *so* tired and to push through fatigue to finish that one last job. I'm seeing younger and younger women getting sick. Many of my coaching clients are overworked, exhausted and overwhelmed.

I'm called to get the message out about the negative impacts on our bodies, minds, and relationships that result from driving ourselves, not listening to our bodies, and living in our left brain. I'm

> *You don't have to live life on the treadmill.*
> ....
> *You can be a High Achieving Woman and at the same time be happy, healthy, and grounded.*

committed to providing tools to prevent other women from becoming exhausted, overcommitted, overwhelmed and seriously ill; tools that provide support as you move toward a balanced life; one that *you* design and love.

You don't have to live life on the treadmill. My book provides proof that there is another healthier way. You *can* be a High Achieving Woman and at the same time be happy, healthy, and grounded.

Why focus this book on women?

* More and more women are becoming leaders, managers and entrepreneurs

- Increasing numbers of women are the primary breadwinners in their families
- Women in all cultures transmit their values and wisdom to their families
- Women have the power to change the world.

Why am I called to write this book now?

A number of people around the world are waking up to the damage caused by greed, competition, self-absorption, and individualism and are adopting the values of contribution, collaboration, connection, and community. More and more women around the globe are stepping into their true power and becoming catalysts for positive change.

In addition:

I believe that humanity is essentially good and
that we are all interconnected.
I believe that everything happens for a reason.
The Universe provides me with what I need and Great
Spirit is guiding me towards fulfillment.
Nature connects me with my soul.

I believe that life is an adventure to be lived to the fullest and that I am here to help build peace in the world.

I developed this faith statement at a personal growth workshop I attended about 15 years ago. I repeat it several times a day and use it to inspire me. I live by all of the above; the statement reflects my core beliefs and guides my interactions with the world.

That said, I struggled for many years trying to make sense of the phrase, *I am here to help build peace in the world.* Then, on May 23, 2013, a light bulb went off in my head. I had listened to a teleseminar that was part of Christine Kloser's *Transformational Author Experience* and suddenly it was as if the key pieces of my life came together and made sense. I understood *why* I am on this journey, *who* I am to serve, and *how* I am to build peace in the world.

In that moment, I realized that I am called to work with women around the globe to enable them to not only find peace within themselves, but to build peace within their families, communities, workplaces, and beyond. We live in a global community connected virtually by the Internet and are also invisibly interconnected, such that when a butterfly flaps its wings in one corner of the world it is felt in another. I believe each and every one of us has the power within us to change the world.

What I've learned from my own journey and work with clients from around the world is that finding peace within results in clarity, focus, and inner contentment. It includes living your passion with ease and grace rather than being constantly in motion and believing that everything has to be a challenge. It means dancing your own dance.

This book shows you how to live and work in different and healthier ways. It invites and supports you to live from the inside out. My hope is that you will learn and grow from the experience of reading this book and engaging in the exercises sprinkled throughout. My intention is to provide you with tools and insights to help you create a healthy, balanced life; one that *you* design and love.

I'd love to hear from you about your experience of reading the book and welcome your questions, comments and feedback at pam@creativelivingcommunity.com.

PART I

High Achieving
Women

Chapter 1

Are You a High Achieving Woman?

Welcome! You are about to embark on a journey. Congratulations on your courage and curiosity!

As part of the process of learning to dance with life, you will uncover and discover aspects of your true self that you may have lost touch with. You will learn proven strategies and powerful practices that connect you with what is really important to you.

Think of this journey as an adventure. As with any adventure, there will be times of uncertainty when you will need to suspend judgment and trust in the process. At other times, you may experience exhilarating energy and *aha* moments. Old habits and fears may rear their heads along the way. Whenever you feel afraid, unprepared, or upset, know that others around the world are with you on the journey. Imagine a global network of interconnected women cheering you on.

In preparation for the journey, I would ask that you open your mind and heart. Believe that you can design your own life. And believe that you can indeed have it all: a life you love, vibrant health, happiness, clarity, fulfillment, and inner peace.

An invitation

As you read this book, I encourage you to journal or audiotape your experiences. Note thoughts and feelings that come up for you along the way. I also recommend that you do the exercises woven throughout the book, as they will assist you on your journey. Please visit *www. creativelivingcommunity.com/workbook/* and download a complimentary workbook that includes all of the exercises, space to record your notes, and additional resources.

Attributes of High Achieving Women

High Achieving Women generally possess a number of attributes in common. Some are positive and some negative. The attributes include:

- Goal-oriented
- Passionate about work
- Organized
- Give more than they receive
- Want to make a difference
- Have trouble saying "no"
- Driven
- Intelligent
- Competitive
- Feel like there are never enough hours in the day
- Self-disciplined
- Achieve more than most in a given time frame
- Perfectionist tendencies; own worst critic
- Love learning
- Creative
- Focus on achievement; never enough
- Rarely take time to bask in the joy of accomplishment
- Courageous
- Spend more time *doing* than *being*

This list is not exhaustive and all High Achieving Women don't possess all of the listed attributes. Based on coaching such women and in-depth interviews and workshops with High Achieving Women, most women who are high achievers possess at least five of the attributes.

> The majority of High Achieving Women tend to give *much more than they* receive, *and many are challenged to reach out for* support. They also spend *much more time* doing *than* being.

The majority of High Achieving Women tend to *give* much more than they *receive,* and many are challenged to reach out for support. They also spend much more time *doing* than *being.*

How many of the attributes on the list apply to you? Out of the entire list, which ones would you categorize as positive and why? Which ones do you view as negative, and why?

Aspects of the attributes

Let's get clear on what we mean by two of the attributes and examine their impacts on our lives, work, health, and relationships.

Attribute: *Give* more than *receive*

Some *giving* behaviors are:

- Listening to a friend's tale of woe
- Making a meal for a sick friend
- Preparing a healthy meal for your partner and/or family
- Volunteering your time to assist others
- Reviewing and editing a friend's resumé
- *Others?*

Some *receiving* behaviors are:

- Treating yourself to a massage or bubble bath
- Eating healthy foods
- Treating yourself to a yoga class and being present during it
- Reaching out for support when you need it: "Honey, do you mind driving the kids to school today?"
- Meditating for at least 10 minutes every day
- *Others?*

If we give more than receive over time we may experience:

- Low energy
- Less patience with and tolerance of others

- Reactivity rather than responsiveness in our inter-actions
- Resentment, or feeling like a victim (I'm always helping Sue but she's never there for me)
- *Others?*

Attribute: Spend much more time doing than being

Some examples of over-doing are:

- Constantly thinking of the next thing that needs to be done
- Hardly ever sitting still
- Nearly always busy; having a packed agenda
- Usually plugged in to technology
- *Others?*

Some examples of *being* are:

- Meditating
- Walking mindfully in nature
- Spending time focusing attentively on someone or something
- *Others?*

What happens in our bodies, minds, and relationships if we spend the majority of our days *doing* rather than *being*?

- We have difficulty focusing on interactions with others as our mind is usually racing and thinking about the next thing we have to do
- We have difficulty sleeping
- We rarely feel a sense of accomplishment at the end of the day
- Our bodies feel tense
- We are usually in "flight", "fight", or "freeze" (the stress response) and our bodies secrete increased amounts of stress hormones such as adrenalin, norepinephrine and cortisol
- We eventually burn out and become ill if we don't slow down and relax
- *Others?*

📖 *Brainstorm a list of the activities you typically do in a day (use yesterday as an example). Go through your list and place a D by the* doing *activities and a B by examples of the* being *activities. Count up the number of activities in each category and the total of both categories. Calculate what percentage of a typical day's activities you spend* doing *and what percentage you spend* being. *Does anything come up for you about this? Are you surprised?*

Based on your observations, commit to integrating at least one new *being* practice into your life on a daily basis and notice how it makes you feel (in your body and in your mind). Notice any impacts this practice has on your relationships at home and at work. Journal about this or record it on your smart phone.

📖 *Imagine how your life would look and feel if you had more of a balance between* doing *and* being. *Visualize that life. Write down how your life would look and the feelings you would experience if you had more balance between* doing *and* being.

Me? A High Achieving Woman?

You may be curious but not sure if you are a High Achieving Woman. If you feel this way, you are not alone. When I conducted interviews with women I consider to be high achieving, some of those selected said things like, *I'm not a High Achieving Woman* or, *I don't have any great accomplishments to my name* or, *I'm not in the corporate world* or, *It sounds arrogant to call myself a High Achieving Woman.*

High Achieving Women are found everywhere: in their own businesses, in corporations, in academia, in government, in not-for-profits. You don't have to be a CEO or a Nobel Prize winner to be a High Achieving Woman, although you may be.

According to Dr. Sherrie Bourg Carter in her book *High Octane Women*, "…it's not status or job title that makes High Achieving Women high achievers. It's how their minds work…how [they] psychologically respond to challenges, which then propels [them] toward excellence in achievement."

Now that you've gone through the list of attributes, you may realize that you are indeed a High Achieving Woman. Even if you're not yet convinced, I encourage you to read on, as the strategies in this book can be beneficial to women from all walks of life.

Some inspiration

I'd like to provide you with inspiration as you embark on your *Creative Living* journey; your conscious journey toward cultivating improved health, happiness, fulfillment, and inner peace. I invite you to read aloud the "Sacred Circles" poem below. As you do so, I encourage you to hold the vision of women around the world supporting you and each other as you move along your path toward vibrant health, happiness, clarity, true fulfillment, and inner peace.

SACRED CIRCLES

We are all women
Connected through the ages.
From hunters and gatherers
To queens and ladies-in-waiting.
Despite our different origins and surroundings,
We all endure similar pain, anxiety, and joy.

Nurturing is what we're known for.
Caring for the sick, the wounded, the children,
Tireless in our cause to improve the lot of humankind.

Sitting in a circle with others, hands clasped,
I feel the energy of powerful women throughout the ages.
I feel their warm blood pulsing through my veins.

The time has come to right the wrongs.
The time has come for women to unite
And be catalysts for peace.
No longer can our voices be hushed.
The time for action has come.

Our feminine qualities of intuition,
warmth, and sensitivity
Enable us to intervene in areas of conflict,
To lead the way towards our vision of a nurturing
and caring world,
A world with love, land, and opportunity
For everyone.

Women in sacred circles have for centuries
felt the energy and
Interconnection among themselves.
Now, more than ever, we need the courage to rise up,
To take action towards making the world
a better place
For our families, friends, neighbors,
And future generations.
Will you accept the challenge?

P. Thompson, October 27, 2000

CHAPTER 2

Preparing for the Journey

A number of women have shared with me how difficult it was for them to "get off the treadmill" and how they felt "out of control" as if an outside force had taken over. One woman exclaimed, *"What is this mechanism that has taken hold of me?"* Another, who has burned out twice, shared:

> *When you're on the wheel you can't stand back enough to get off....I kept thinking,* I want to get off the wheel, why can't I do it?*....I couldn't figure out how to do it...had I not been pushed off [given a severance package] I would have stayed on....My family had been bugging me for two years...I kept putting it off. Suddenly one day, I [realized] they*

were right....The process was long....We can't get off
[the treadmill] even when we know it's bad [for us].

Twila

The journey from living life on a treadmill to being able to dance with life doesn't happen overnight. It takes time, along with courage, commitment, and openness to learning and growing. In the words of Dr. Valencia Ray, consultant and executive coach, speaker and trainer, "It's like peeling off the layers of an onion....It's a dance in which you engage your intellect and your intuition."

> *The journey from living life on a treadmill to being able to dance with life doesn't happen overnight. It takes time, along with courage, commitment, and openness to learning and growing.*

To assist you in preparing for the journey, it's helpful to explore change and how you respond to it.

Responding to change

We live in an increasingly complex world where change is all around us; in fact, one of the only constants in our lives is change. And we all react and respond to change differently.

How have you responded in the past to changes in your life? Reflecting on this will provide clues as to how you might respond to consciously integrating new behaviors into your life, and to changing old patterns of behavior. Another point to acknowledge as you consider your response to change is whether or not the change has been forced upon you (being fired as opposed to resigning).

On a scale of 1 to 10, (with 1 being "thrive on it" and 10 being "scares me to death") how would you rate your usual reaction to change? Can you explain how you typically respond to a change experience?

Reflecting on past experiences with life changes, what have you learned that has supported you to adapt and move forward positively?

Barriers to change/moving forward

A number of barriers to change have been identified, including:

- Becoming paralyzed by fear
- Procrastinating
- Blaming others
- Believing we can't do something, or that we are not worthy
- Focusing on problems rather than solutions
- Getting stuck in old habits or denying change is happening
- Being unwilling to put in the effort required to make a change

What barriers do you have to integrating more being *behaviors into your life? To consciously implementing new ways of receiving? To celebrating and nurturing yourself on a regular basis? Take a few minutes to jot down your responses to these questions.*

Overcoming resistance to change

M. J. Ryan, in her book *Adaptability: How to Survive Change You Didn't Ask For* (2009), notes that the ability to adapt is "the key indicator of success in these turbulent times. It's the capacity to be flexible and resourceful in the face of ever-changing conditions."

Aikido masters say that to be successful in life three types of mastery are needed: mastery with self; mastery with others; and mastery with change, meaning "the capacity to adapt easily without losing our center – our values, talents and sense of purpose." (Ryan, 2009).

How can we learn to recover quickly from change and be adaptable so that when we choose to make a change or change is forced upon us we view it as an opportunity?

There are a number of studies and tools in the literature that provide us with a better understanding of change and how to navigate it successfully. Maddi and Kobassa, in their book *Resilience at Work: How to Succeed No Matter What Life Throws You* (2005), analyzed data from 400 studies on organizational change and also conducted their own study of AT&T executives during a corporate reorganization. They found that those who thrived while undergoing organizational change displayed certain character traits, which they called the 3Cs. They identified these as:

- Challenge
- Control
- Commitment.

By challenge, the authors meant that the individual saw change as an opportunity to learn and grow, and was optimistic about the future. Control meant the individuals believed that they had choices and could influence their lives and events around them. Rather than worrying about things they could *not* control, they focused on identifying what they could influence and took action on those things. Commitment meant the individuals lived their lives passionately and stayed connected to people even when times got tough.

Tips to help you embrace change and move forward

1. Change your perspective. View change as an opportunity: for self-growth and learning; for exploring new solutions and ways of doing things; for "putting on a new pair of glasses" and seeing the world differently.

2. Slow down and go inside yourself. Instead of keeping yourself busy, create some time and space for yourself each day. Set aside time in your schedule for you. Spend at least 30 minutes a day meditating, journaling, walking in nature, *being.*

3. Get in touch with and acknowledge your feelings. Don't push away your feelings; experience them. This allows the process of healing from the inside out to begin.

4. Express those feelings. Draw, journal, paint, dance…

5. Express gratitude regularly. Create a gratitude journal or write down at least five things you are grateful for each morning or evening. Research shows that people who express appreciation and gratitude on a regular basis are more optimistic and lead happier lives.

6. Believe in yourself. Think of all the positive things you've accomplished in the past. Recall a particular time you felt really proud of what you'd done and then connect with the positive feelings you felt at that time.

> *View change as an opportunity: for self-growth and learning; for exploring new solutions and ways of doing things; for "putting on a new pair of glasses" and seeing the world differently.*

7. Nurture and take care of yourself. Make sure you eat well, get enough sleep, and exercise regularly. Do something special for yourself on occasion, such as going for a massage, having a bubble bath, buying a new outfit; remember you are special and deserve the best.

8. Reach out for support. Ask a friend, counselor, or life coach to help you. Surround yourself with people who believe in you and are not judgmental. This may involve changing your friends and those you spend time with.

9. Identify the things you can control when you're going through change. Choosing what you think (thoughts), how you speak (language), and what you say (stories) influences the change (from Ariane de Bonvoisin, *the first 30 days*).

PART II

Learning to Dance with Life

CHAPTER 3

Creative Living and the Seven Keys

I learned at a young age from my family that working hard, setting goals, and achieving were important. My father set the bar high and praised us for our accomplishments. As a result, I have always given 110% to my studies and various careers.

Early in my professional life, I had a number of interesting positions but never stayed for many years in any of them. Then, when I founded my own process/ management consulting company, *InPro Consulting*, in 1992, I discovered the joy of having my own business.

I love to travel and learn about different countries and cultures, and had always dreamed of working internationally. In 2003, I joined an international development consulting group and managed several large projects in Asia and Africa. In 2007, I founded a second consulting company, *Global Village Consulting,* which enabled me to use my varied skill-set for clients in North America and in the developing world.

In 2008, I studied through Leadership University to become a life and business coach and launched *Creative Life Coaching Inc.* Soon after, I founded the Creative Healing Centre, a virtual organization where coaching, healing, and the arts came together.

I've had some amazing opportunities during my life: being commissioned by the Pan American Health Organization to write a document entitled *Health Promotion: Improving the Health Status of Women and Promoting Equity*; being part of a World Health Organization delegation to Russia just after the Berlin Wall came down; and living and working in Kabul, Afghanistan as Technical Advisor to the Ministry of Public Health from mid-October 2010 to mid-November 2011.

I worked night and day for many years and had lots of energy. Then in late 2010, things started to change. While in Afghanistan, I got pneumonia twice and started to get recurring bladder infections. I was passionate about the work, so I kept up an intense pace and didn't listen to my body. This continued into 2012 when I signed a one-year contract with an NGO that promotes women's and children's rights around the world.

Part way through the year-long contract, I began to lose my passion. I started to feel *so* tired. When my client asked me to negotiate a new contract for 2013 I came close to signing, but asked if I could sleep on it. When I woke up the next day, my body felt so bad, like a lemon that had been squeezed dry. I realized I needed to take a break. I thanked my client for the opportunity and declined the offer. When asked why, I said I wanted *to create more balance in my life.*

I spent much of 2013 focusing on creating balance. I studied and experimented with various tools and techniques from neuroscience, Eastern psychology, and the business literature on working smart. I started to meditate daily, used mindfulness practices, practiced yoga four to five times a week, spent more time in nature, and consciously spent more time connecting with family and friends. I also slept 10 to 12 hours a night for about three months — and was still tired. In April I consulted a naturopath who diagnosed toxins in my liver, adrenal glands, and kidneys. She prescribed a number of homeopathic remedies.

By mid-May 2013 I was starting to feel more like myself and began to write the book on *Creative Living* that had been in my head since 2008.

> *Creative Living is the conscious cultivation of improved health and happiness, fulfillment, and inner peace in your life.*

What is Creative Living?

Creative Living is the conscious cultivation of improved health and happiness, fulfillment, and inner peace in your life. The seven elements of *Creative Living* are:

1.   Body wisdom
2.   Creativity
3.   Balance
4.   Core values
5.   Beliefs
6.   Life transitions
7.   Inner peace

The elements may be likened to seeds that germinate when nourished with sufficient water, food, and warmth. The "work" that we do around each seed enables us to cultivate a unique garden of health, happiness, fulfillment, and peace.

Each element has one key associated with it. The keys assist us in opening the doors to our true selves. The seven keys to *Creative Living* are:

1. Listen to and trust in your body's wisdom
2. Tap into and express your creative side
3. Consciously create right and left brain/body balance
4. Live life in alignment with your core values
5. Believe that you are here to make a difference
6. Learn from and embrace life transitions
7. Find inner peace, and build peace in your family, friends, community, workplace…the world.

The value of growing your practice of the seven keys is supported by evidence from neuroscience, the arts, and Eastern psychology. I've learned from personal experience and from working with clients that integrating the seven keys to *Creative Living* into your life will support you as you learn to dance with life.

Each chapter in this section is devoted to one of the seven keys. Each one includes the components of each key, why they are important, the supporting evidence, and proven strategies and powerful practices to assist you to integrate them into your life.

CHAPTER 4

Key #1 - Listen To and Trust in Your Body's Wisdom

Since I was quite young I have known the power of listening to my body. And as I reflect on my life, I realize that the decisions I made from my heart or my gut have always been the right ones for me, resulting in positive life experiences. When the decisions came solely from my head and my logical left brain (using a pros and cons list), the results were not so good.

During the last 15 years or so I have become consciously aware of how important it is to listen to the body, and how to do it. This chapter is about reconnecting with the body, and learning how to tap into, listen to, and trust in its wisdom.

The importance of cultivating a healthy body, mind, and spirit

> *The mind cannot function very well if the body is not healthy. Our ability to think, reason, create, etc., is greatly diminished when the attention and focus of our minds is directed to a health problem....When we are feeling well, however, the body becomes the perfect instrument for allowing the mind and spirit to focus on its tasks, and for experiencing the almost magical effects that come from a creative mind and a free spirit.*
>
> Austin Vickers, 2005

There is increasing evidence of the negative impacts on our body that come from not listening to the messages it sends us. Gabor Maté, in *When the Body Says No (2003),* provides case studies and research evidence linking stress with cancer and auto-immune disorders. Ruth Buczynski writes in a blog post that the high stress of our complicated lives "can wreak havoc on our brain's ability to control emotions, maintain focus and perform tasks" (NICABM blog post December 10, 2013- http://

www.nicabm.com/nicabmblog/the-brain-under-stress-using-mindfulness-to-regain-focus/).

> As I reflect on my life, I realize that the decisions I made from my heart or my gut have always been the right ones for me, resulting in positive life experiences. When the decisions came solely from my head and my logical left-brain (using a pros and cons list), the results were not so good.

Yet how often have you pushed through fatigue to get that document done or client request met?

How can we moderate the ways we respond to stress, and improve our health? In addition to getting seven to eight hours of healing sleep a night and consuming healthful foods, there are a number of proven tools and strategies that support a healthy body, mind, and spirit.

Becoming consciously aware of our bodies

Have you noticed how you often feel extremely full after a holiday meal? Feeling so full is uncomfortable. You tell yourself that you will never have a second helping again.

Have you sensed tension and stress when you walk into certain organizations or situations? We often say, "You could cut the air with a knife."

Have you noticed that when you're interacting with certain individuals you feel tense and can't wait to leave their presence? These are all examples of our bodies warning us and trying to keep us safe.

On the other hand, have you ever been with someone who makes you feel appreciated and happy in his or her presence? Have you been in an organization, on a team, or in a situation where you felt valued and respected?

Our bodies are amazing receivers and transmitters of information. Integrating tools and strategies that bring conscious awareness into our lives can improve the health of body, mind, and spirit.

Tools to help you enhance body awareness

Body Scan

A body scan is an excellent tool to use when we wish to bring more awareness to our body and the messages it sends us. Body scanning is a mindfulness technique from

Eastern psychology that is rooted in Buddhist principles. Mindfulness itself is a practice that teaches us to focus on feeling sensations and emotions in our body, and notice what is going on in our mind. The practice cultivates within us the ability to live "in the present moment." By performing a body scan, we take time to notice and feel our body's sensations.

Sit comfortably, close your eyes, and take several deep breaths in through your nose and out through your mouth. Then return to regular breathing; in through your nose, and out through your nose.

From a state of open and relaxed awareness begin scanning your body from the top of your head to the tips of your toes. Notice any sensations you feel (without judging them) from your scalp, forehead, ears, eyes, nose, cheeks, and mouth. Then move down through the rest of your body. You may scan several times from head to toe in one sitting, or, after scanning once, attend to places in your body where you feel the most sensation. Experiment with this tool and find the process that is most useful for you. This may be done first thing in the morning and/or at night before you retire. It also may be done at various other times during the day.

There is another way to use the body scan. If you notice tension in your body, focus on and breathe into the tense area(s). As you breathe out, focus on releasing the tension. Do this a few times until the tension in your body reduces or goes away. Focusing on tension or pain and breathing into it, rather than pushing it away and trying to avoid it, has been shown to be effective in reducing both pain and tension.

Body scanning may be used as a tool to bring awareness to what happens in your body when you feel stressed, angry, criticized, happy, or excited. Tara Brach, in her book *Radical Acceptance: Embracing Your Life with the Heart of a Buddha* (2003), walks you through a detailed body scan and explains its power.

You may find it useful to view and listen to Stephen Cope's body scan meditation on YouTube. http://www.youtube.com/watch?v=QgmabXt_UU8&feature=youtube_gdata_player -

Walking Meditation

A tool that I have found extremely useful for helping me to get out of my head and into my body is mindfulness walking meditation. When we do a mindfulness walking meditation outdoors, we feel the ground beneath our feet, the breeze against our face, and the cool air flowing through our nostrils down into our lungs. We smell the scent of salt or the aroma of lavender in the air, and we observe the scenery around us. We try to stay out of our mind, and experience our senses. Rather than spending our time constantly thinking about and processing all the things we have to do, we stay present and experience all of nature's beautiful sights, smells, sounds, and sensations.

Walking meditation can also be practiced indoors.

Evidence of the benefits of mindfulness practices

The National Institute for the Clinical Application of Behavioral Medicine (NICABM) offers a number of excellent free courses and teleseminars on mindfulness. They cite evidence that mindfulness practice:

- Positively changes brain structure and function
- Increases brain activity associated with positive feelings
- Shrinks the amygdala – the part of our brain that triggers our fight-or-flight response
- Increases the brain waves associated with neural integration and well-being
- Leads to an increased sense of well-being, not to mention greater stress resilience and deeper empathy in both professional and personal relationships
- Improves attention, learning, and memory
- Measurably increases compassionate behavior
- Decreases the frequency and severity of stress, and the symptoms that come with it, including inflammatory bowel disease, insomnia, and sexual dysfunction
- Correlates with reduced feelings of burnout and increased stress resilience
- Reduces experiences of pain, including chronic pain

(http://www.nicabm.com/
mindfulnessandpsychotherapy2013/a2-
info/?del=plcredirect)

Neuroplasticity

Strong evidence from neuroscience demonstrates that we can change the physiology of our brains by our thoughts. Norman Doidge, in his book *The Brain that Changes Itself* (2007), shares incredible stories and evidence of the power of our minds to change our brains. However, he cautions that neuroplasticity "... renders our brains not only more resourceful but also more vulnerable to outside influences....Neuroplasticity has the power to produce more flexible but also more rigid behaviors."

Enhancing the ability to focus on the positive

As High Achieving Women, many of us rarely take the time to celebrate ourselves or bask in the pleasure of our accomplishments. But lessons from neuroscience show that reflecting on the positive is important for our well-being.

In *Hardwiring Happiness* (2013), neuropsychologist Rick Hanson explains why our brains are like "velcro for negative experiences" and "Teflon for positive ones." Human brains have evolved with a negativity bias that makes us "overestimate threats and underestimate opportunities and resources." Hanson provides evidence that the "best way to compensate for the negativity bias is to regularly take in the good."

You can do this by taking time to smile and think positive thoughts before getting out of bed in the morning. Perhaps bring to mind a song that energizes you, or a picture of someone you love. Set the intention that your day will be good. Then notice how your day rolls out.

In contrast, reflect on those days when you hit the ground running, already thinking of everything that could go wrong in the day ahead as you wake up. Reflect on how those days went. Being consciously aware of our thoughts and choosing to focus on the positive have powerful impacts on our lives.

At the end of each day, I encourage you to get still and think about one thing that you did during the day that you would like to celebrate. It can be big or small. The important thing is to identify something, state it aloud, and feel the celebration in your body. It may initially feel foreign for you to do this but it is a practice I've found to be extremely helpful for clients and for me.

The link between heart, gut, and brain

Did you know that our gut and our heart have nerve endings that send signals to our brains? So when we say that our gut or heart is telling us something, there is scientific evidence that this is so.

Our primitive brain is the part of the brain that enabled us to survive from caveman days. When we experience stress, it releases hormones (such as adrenaline, norepinephrine and cortisol) that put our body into a "fight or flight" response. Our heart races, blood flow shifts from our skin to our large muscles, and we are enabled to run fast or stand and fight if we need to. The amygdala, which resides in the primitive part of the brain, protects us. Yet it also controls us. It's the part of our unconscious mind that often reacts when we find ourselves in new situations.

The sympathetic nervous system has evolved to protect us for short periods of time by flooding us with fight or flight hormones. Then it stops producing the stress hormones so that our body can return to balance, or homeostasis. When we are under chronic stress from our jobs, relationships, or other things, the sympathetic nervous system doesn't get a message to "stop the flow."

The stress hormones continue to be secreted and our body can't return to homeostasis. This inability to "relax" leads to increased blood pressure and blood sugar, a suppressed immune system, and reduced libido, among other less-than-desirable health impacts.

It is important to notice when your body becomes reactive and to ask yourself why you are reacting in this way. For example, ask yourself, *Is this person or situation really to be feared or is it my body feeling uncomfortable with something or someone new and trying to protect me based on past experience?* When you take the time to notice that your body is reacting, and then check in with it, you can consciously choose how you respond, rather than allowing yourself to be unconsciously controlled by a primitive system that was developed to protect you from external threats.

How can you access, listen to, and trust in your body's wisdom and the messages it sends you?

Getting in touch with your body's wisdom

At first when you "go inside" and ask for guidance, you may be uncertain about whether you are really listening to your body's wisdom or whether it is your ego or logical left brain "speaking" to you. To enable you to get in touch with your body and its "inner knowing," the following strategies are helpful.

1. **Practice yoga regularly,** at least three times a week. There are a myriad of types of yoga available. Yin yoga is a good place to start, particularly if you have an extremely active mind that rarely stops chattering. Yin has a meditative quality, is usually done in a warm room and involves holding poses for up to five minutes so that connective tissue loosens and energy blocks release. If you are already doing yoga but haven't yet tried yin, I recommend trying it at least twice a week for a month and noticing if you experience any changes in your body and mind. If you view yoga mostly as a form of physical exercise, spend more time during the classes focusing on your body, and notice how it feels before, during and after each class.

2. **Meditate daily** for at least ten minutes. For years people told me about the benefits of meditating

regularly, but it wasn't until January 2013 that I began doing it on a consistent basis. I have to say I am amazed by the benefits. Meditation enables me to be less reactive and more responsive in my interactions with others. I've noticed that at times it enables my brain to "split," so that while I'm engaged in an interaction I also experience part of myself "sitting on my shoulder" observing the interaction. This provides me with the big picture and helps me to stay calm and detached from the outcome. I have found the 21-day meditation challenges (CDs and MP3s) available through www.chopra.com helpful in practicing meditation and learning to focus on one concept or idea.

During meditation, if you find that your mind is really active and it's difficult to sit still, try a walking meditation. You can do this inside a building or outside in nature. To begin, lift one foot and slowly press heel then toes on the ground. Follow with the other foot, being totally present with your movements rather than thinking about all you have to do or reviewing a recent argument with your significant other. Continue with walking meditation for as long as you like.

If you find that a painful emotion comes up during meditation, notice it, breathe into it, and investigate. What does it look like? What color, consistency, or feeling does it have (for example, black, thick like mud, heavy)? Take the emotion outside your body. Befriend it. Thank it for protecting you. Imagine it being inside a balloon or bubble and release it; imagine it floating away from you up into the sky.

3. **Nurture your body** on a regular basis. One thing I like to do is to have a total body massage from a trusted practitioner and during the massage ask what he or she notices about my body. Some massage therapists are also healers and energy workers. They can assist in releasing energy blocks and balancing energy. Therapists can also help you to go within and get in touch with your body and what it's telling you.

A while ago, I asked my massage therapist (who is also a healer) what she noticed about my body that day. She said that my left side was much tighter than my right side. She also said that the right side was my "giving" side and the left side was my "receiving" side. I had an *aha* moment. I realized that I give a lot more than I receive and my body was speaking to me about that. Massage assisted in releasing energy blocks in the left side of my body and also provided me with a clue about how I could live a healthier life.

Ask yourself what you would really like to do to reward or nurture yourself, and listen to what comes up for you. I've noticed that having a hot tub or a bubble bath in a candle-lit room with pleasant music playing in the background relaxes and nurtures me. When I let go of all the noise and stress of the day, I notice my body relax. Then I can go inside and truly listen to what my body wants to tell me.

Using your body to make wise decisions

What I've found is that if I don't listen to my body over time, it whacks me on the side of the head in order

> *What I've found is that if I don't listen to my body over time, it whacks me on the side of the head in order to get my attention.*

to get my attention. An example is an experience from my marriage.

For a number of years I hadn't been happy in my relationship. Yet I was enjoying working hard, and had a handsome husband who earned good money. I could travel whenever I wanted to and had two amazing children. From the outside it appeared that I "had it all." Yet often when I stopped (which was rarely) thoughts of leaving my marriage surfaced. So I would get busy working, push those thoughts down, and avoid making any changes.

Some years went by. I was given the opportunity to join my husband in Barbados on my way back from a business trip to Nigeria. It was a rare treat to be able to fit in my business with his travel. I was so looking forward to ten days of rest and relaxation. Within the first 24 hours of my arrival, I got a strong message. My inner wisdom told me that I had to leave my husband. When I asked when, I was told, "by your 50th birthday." It was May and I was turning 50 in September of the same year! I realized at that moment that if I didn't leave my marriage, my soul would die.

Within two weeks I had told my husband that I couldn't grow old with him and began to make preparations to separate from a marriage I'd been in for 24 years. After making and acting on that life-changing decision I felt so much lighter, as though a ball and chain had been released from my legs. I "knew" it was the right thing to do.

How can you listen to and hear what your body is telling you? Can you trust that your body makes decisions that are for your highest good and act on them, rather than continuing to avoid making changes to situations and relationships that are no longer serving you?

Think about a decision you would like assistance in making. Get comfortable, close your eyes, take several deep breaths in through your nose and out through your mouth. Then continue to breathe normally in and out through your nose. Feel your feet and imagine roots coming out of the bottom of them and reaching deep down into Mother

Earth. Imagine your shoulders and head growing branches that reach up to the sky and tap into the beautiful Source Energy/God/Universal Energy (whatever you choose to call it). Feel that light coming in through the top of your head and bathing your entire body. Now that you are grounded and connected with earth and sky/heavens, ask the question that you would like clarity on. It could be, Should I apply for that new position? Should I have an enrollment conversation with that person? *Continue to breathe deeply and notice if any answers come up for you. Some people experience a sense of knowing, others receive an auditory message, still others see a vision of someone speaking to them, or an object that is a metaphor or a sign of what is in their best interest or for the highest good.*

This takes time and practice. Be patient with yourself and learn to trust the process and your body's wisdom. You may find it easier to start with smaller decisions that don't involve much change in your life: *Should I call up my friend today*? Often when you follow your heart or gut and call up a friend, they will say to you, "We must have ESP!" or, "I was just thinking of you and about to give you a call." It's like a muscle: the more you use your body's wisdom, the easier it will become and in time you will make decisions that you trust are the right ones for you.

Some people find that initially no answer comes to them. If you find that to be the case, don't beat yourself up. Rather, ask throughout the day for a sign that provides you with the answer. Let go and get on with your day and notice that at some time when you're not thinking about it, the answer may come to you and you will know what action to take.

> *It's like a muscle: the more you use your body's wisdom, the easier it will become and in time you will make decisions that you trust are the right ones for you.*

Another suggestion is to ask a question just before you go to sleep at night and also ask that you receive the answer on awakening. It's helpful to keep a pen and paper by your bed in case things come to you during the night or on awakening.

Energy and energy management

Have you noticed that interactions with certain people leave you feeling drained physically and emotionally? Have you been in environments and/or organizations where your body feels tense and unsafe?

Becoming aware of your own energy levels and how certain individuals and environments affect them is important for your health and well-being. In the words of energy psychiatrist Judith Orloff:

> *...you need to pinpoint and eliminate influences that diminish you. Or if you can't avoid them, discover how to protect yourself....When you embrace the positive and say "no" to the negative, high energy and optimism become a choice.*
>
> Orloff, *Positive Energy*

It is said that we are like the five people we spend the most time with.

🎁 *Write down the five people you spend the most time with. They may be friends, colleagues and/or family members. Generally, how do you feel when you are in each of these people's presence? How do you feel when you leave them? Jot these feelings or emotions down by each one. Think about which people affect you positively and negatively. Notice how they affect you in body, mind, and spirit. How do they influence your feelings of self-worth, your perspective on the world, your productivity, and your interactions with others? Note the impacts they have.*

Make a decision to spend less time with those people who negatively affect your energy and in environments that drain your energy. If you are working in a particularly stressful environment and/or with people who negatively affect your energy, it is helpful, before you leave home, to close your eyes and imagine you are surrounded by a protective bubble. What I say to myself is, "Guide and protect me as I move through today. Surround me with a protective bubble and if any negative energy, hooks, or barbs come my way may they bounce off and return to sender as love, light, and healing energy."

You may also (in your office or workspace) surround yourself with things that give you pleasure, such as plants, family photos, a nature calendar, or subdued lighting. Notice what particular things in your environment make you feel calm and relaxed and surround yourself with them.

Managing your inner landscape

As High Achieving Women, many of us are hard on our selves; we are our own worst critic and we have perfectionistic tendencies. It is important to become aware of our inner critic or inner perfectionist and any associated negative self-talk and take steps to replace it with positive self-talk.

Here are a few strategies for managing your inner landscape.

1. Celebrate yourself and your achievements on a regular basis.
2. Keep a gratitude journal. Write down at least five things you are grateful for at the beginning and/or end of each day.
3. Be compassionate with yourself. thefreedictionary. com defines compassion as "deep awareness of the suffering of another coupled with the wish to relieve it." There are a number of forms of compassion med-

itation to help you to become more compassionate with yourself and with others. I particularly like Jack Kornfield's approach (e.g. http://www.jackkornfield. com/meditation-on-compassion/).

4. Be patient with yourself. Joan Borysenko, in her book *Inner Peace for Busy People,* defines patience as "a gentle willingness to let life unfold at its own pace." She recommends noticing the times when you are impatient and asking yourself, "What's the hurry?" Think about what you'll lose by doing something quickly and what you'll gain by savoring the moment and being truly mindful and focused on what you are doing. Borysenko also notes that "learning to be patient is a continual practice that takes years to ripen. Let it unfold, day by day, and be gentle with yourself in the learning."

Conclusion

Listening to and trusting in your body's wisdom is the foundational key to improving your health, and to finding happiness, true fulfillment and inner peace. If you're being challenged with getting in touch with and trusting in your body's wisdom and you'd like support, I encourage you to visit http://creativelivingcommunity.com/coaching/ and/or email support@creativeliving-community.com to learn more about our one-on-one and group coaching programs.

CHAPTER 5

Key#2 - Tap into and Express Your Creative Side

Creativity is in the soul of our being and our highest form of living. It is the presence within all of us that relentlessly longs for expression.

Suzanne Kyra, *Welcome Home to Yourself*

How many adults believe that they are not creative? A number of my clients, friends, and colleagues remember a particular skill or talent they practiced regularly as children, such as drawing, writing, painting, or dancing. A gift that when practiced they got lost in and forgot about time. And they felt truly happy when the practice was complete. When asked why they stopped using their particular talent, many said a parent or influential adult in their life told them not to waste their time as they would never make a living doing that, or to get on with studying more important things so that they could become a doctor, lawyer, teacher…and make money.

> In Western culture today, knowledge and information are generally highly valued and creativity and the arts undervalued. Many of us are so plugged in and challenged to keep up with all of our emails, text messages, blogs, and so on that we do not take time to tap into and express our creativity.

In Western culture today, knowledge and information are generally highly valued and creativity and the arts undervalued. Many of us are so plugged in and challenged to keep up with all of our emails, text messages, blogs, and so on that we do not take time to tap into and express our creativity.

As Suzanne's quote eloquently states, we are all creative beings who long to express ourselves. Danny Gregory, in his book *The Creative License* (2006), states that "the ability and need to be creative are hard-wired into all of us." He notes that we need to give ourselves permission to be the artists we truly are. Gregory cautions that when we stifle our creativity "our minds grow narrower...we grow remote from others, categorizing and stereotyping the people we meet...we speed through life, wanting to get on to the next thing, unable to take pleasure in the moment."

At *Creative Life* Coaching, we value creativity and believe that we are all creative beings with unique gifts. We also believe that linking artistic pursuits with alternative types of healing promotes and supports health and wellness, and that getting in touch with our creative self leads to wholeness.

The right brain, and left brain

The right side of the brain is associated with creativity, emotion, "big picture" thinking and intuition, whereas the left brain is associated with logic, structure, words, language, and rational thought. We all draw on both sides of the brain for a variety of daily tasks, but we are usually either right- or left-brain dominant. An example of someone who is left-brain dominant would be a person who is orderly, logical, and analytical.

Someone who is right-brain dominant is more emotional, creative, and adventurous.

Reconnect with your right brain and tap into your creativity by taking up a hobby you may have enjoyed as a child. Or try an artistic pursuit that is completely new, such as pottery. Many people report that engaging in watercolor painting, making pottery, or drawing, for example, makes them feel relaxed, takes their mind off work, and in some cases, feel like a child at play.

A number of years ago I decided it would be fun to make pottery gifts for friends and family, so I signed up for classes at a local studio. I remember being in awe when the instructor did the demonstration and transformed a ball of clay into a beautiful object within a few moments. When I got my own ball of clay and started to create something on the potter's wheel, I noticed the chatter leave my head. I got lost in the moment, felt like a child at play and was able to totally focus on what I was creating (otherwise there would have been a blob of clay on my wheel or on the floor!).

The importance of laughter and play

Many of us have heard that laughter is the best medicine. When we laugh, we release endorphins and encourage energy to move throughout our body. In the words of Candace Pert, a neuroscientist and pharmacologist who spent much of her scientific life studying the mind-body link:

> *Play and laughter are vital to feeling good. Recreation isn't merely a frivolous addition to life or a hard-earned reward for work...I believe that in a society driven by a strong work ethic, with so many individuals burdened with workaholism, people aren't getting enough endorphinergic surges through the bodymind on a regular basis. For you to not be laughing and playing during some part of every day is unnatural and goes against your fundamental biochemistry.*

Everything You Need to Feel Go(o)d, 2006

Stuart Brown, founder of the National Institute for Play, has conducted research that shows play is not only energizing and fun, but also important for human physical, emotional, and cognitive development, and intelligence. (http://www.nifplay.org) His YouTube video outlines different types of play and provides evidence of the importance of play throughout our lives. http://www.ted.com/talks/stuart_brown_says_play_is_more_than_fun_it_s_vital.html

> Based on the research by Brown, Pert, and others, it is recommended for the health of our minds and bodies that we engage in play and laughter every day.

Based on the research by Brown, Pert, and others, it is recommended for the health of our minds and bodies that we engage in play and laughter every day.

Alexandra Jaye Johnson, in her article "How to be More Playful and Have More Fun," identifies 10 Big Ideas related to being playful and having fun. https://www.entheos.com/academy/classes/how-to-be-a-fun-and-playful-goddess/entheos

Play includes jumping, skipping, making a snow-man, tickling or being tickled, being curious, or creating and sharing a fantasy story with a child.

Here are a few suggestions of how to integrate more play and laughter into your life.

Identify and write down types of play activities you enjoyed and engaged in as a child.

2. *Reflect on how many of these activities you currently engage in as an adult and how often you engage in them.*

3. *Rate on a scale of 1 to 10 how energized each of the above activities makes you feel – 1 being "not at all" and 10 being "full of energy".*

4. *Identify several play activities you would like to begin integrating into your life. Experiment and notice how they make you feel.*

5. *Commit to engaging in some form of play or laughter on a daily basis. Ask friends and family for support (perhaps make it a family project to laugh and play at least once a day) and encourage play and laughter in their lives as well.*

Whole-brain thinking

With the increasing complexity of big issues, such as climate change and new strains of flu, and the rapid rate of technological change we are experiencing, authors such as Ken Robinson (in *The Element)* and

Daniel Pink (in *A Whole New Mind)* are making the case that we need to shift our emphasis away from valuing mainly left-brain traits/functions. They encourage us to change educational systems and organizations so that they stimulate, encourage, and reward the right-brain functions of creativity and innovation.

Pink believes we are moving from the Information Age to the Conceptual Age, a new age that requires a different way of thinking and a whole new approach to life and work. Pink emphasizes that to lead a successful and healthy life we need to use both sides of the brain. He calls this whole-brain thinking.

During the Information Age, left-brain thinking was most valued. In the new Conceptual Age, using right-brain abilities will be necessary for success. Pink provides hard data on the economic and social forces that are changing our work environments. The Conceptual Age is one of "high concept" and "high touch." In the future, being successful in business will require six abilities that Pink refers to as *Design, Story, Symphony, Empathy, Play, and Meaning.*

Design

Design is "high concept." In the Conceptual Age it is no longer sufficient to create a functional product, service, or experience. It is crucial to create products, services, and experiences that are beautiful, fun, or emotionally engaging.

Story

Storytelling "…is a key way for individuals and entrepreneurs to distinguish their goods and services in a crowded marketplace." It is important to understand yourself and what you offer as well as your target market(s) and create compelling and persuasive stories that communicate your uniqueness.

Symphony

"Synthesis, seeing the big picture, crossing boundaries, and being able to combine disparate pieces into an arresting new whole" is what is important in this new age.

Empathy

Empathy is the ability to relate to what someone is experiencing and feeling, and to make a connection with them. "What will distinguish those who thrive will be their ability to understand what makes their fellow woman or man tick, to forge relationships, and to care for others."

Play

Laughter, humor, and play in and out of the workplace are important and foster health and well-being.

Meaning

Having so much material abundance around us has freed us to pursue the drive we all have to find purpose and meaning in all aspects of our lives.

According to Pink, "anyone can master the six Conceptual Age senses. But those who master them first will have a huge advantage."

Take a few minutes now to examine Pink's six Conceptual Age senses.

Ask yourself the following questions:

📖 *How am I at designing things? Do I enjoy design? What sorts of design work do I enjoy? Some examples include designing buildings, courses, gardens, jewelry, or furniture. Rate yourself on a scale of 1 to 10 (1 being "not at all" and 10 being "I rock in this area") in terms of how much a part of your current life and way of living design is and how you are at it. If you rated yourself as 7 or more, well done. If you rated yourself as less than 7, what things might you do to strengthen your interest and skills in design?*

2. *How am I at storytelling? Rate yourself on a scale of 1 to 10 in terms how good you are at it and how much a part of your life it is (1 being "so bad"/"not at all" and 10 being "I rock in this area").*

3. *Ask yourself similar questions related to Symphony, Empathy, Play, and Meaning, and rate yourself. If you rate yourself less than a 7 in any areas, think about how you might strengthen your knowledge and skills in those areas.*

The arts, health, and healing

There is a lot of evidence supporting the value of the arts in promoting health and enhancing healing. James Pennebaker, in his book *Writing to Heal: A guided journal for recovering from trauma and emotional upheaval*

> There is a lot of evidence supporting the value of the arts in promoting health and enhancing healing.

(2004), notes, "The evidence is mounting that the act of writing about traumatic experience for as little as fifteen to twenty minutes a day for three or four days can produce measurable changes in physical and mental health." Laura Cerwinske in her book *Writing as Healing Art* (1999) states that "the power of the written word stimulates the flow of emotions and readily opens the door to the subconscious." She provides a number of processes and "assignments" for using writing as a way to heal ourselves and to tap into our creativity. Julia Cameron in *The Artist's Way: A Spiritual Path to Higher Creativity* (1992) describes the importance of learning to "recognize, nurture and protect your inner artist (and in so doing)...you will learn ways to recognize and resolve fear, remove emotional scar tissue, and strengthen your confidence."

The National Center for Creative Aging (NCCA) was founded by Dr. Eugene Cohen in 2001. The NCCA is dedicated to fostering an understanding of the vital relationship between creative expression and healthy aging, and to developing programs that build on this understanding.

Dr. Cohen's research demonstrates that creative expression is important for older people of all cultures and ethnic backgrounds, regardless of economic status, age, or level of physical, emotional, or cognitive functioning. The process of aging is a profound experience marked by physical and emotional changes and a heightened search for meaning and purpose. The arts can serve as a powerful way to engage elders in a creative and healing process of self-expression, enabling them to create works that honor their life experience. (www.creativeaging.org)

Tap into your creativity

Shaun McNiff is an artist and art therapist. In his book *Art Heals: How Creativity Cures the Soul* (2004) he articulates from his experience:

> *I have consistently discovered that the core process of healing through art involves the cultivation and release of the creative spirit. If we can liberate the*

creative process in our lives, it will always find the way to whatever needs attention and transformation. The challenge, then is first to free our creativity and then to sustain it as a disciplined practice.

How do you cultivate and release your creative spirit?

Sit down in a quiet place, free from distractions. Take a few deep breaths to relax yourself and close your eyes for a couple of minutes if you feel comfortable doing so. Ask yourself the following questions and write down your responses to them. Write down the first thing that comes to mind without judging or editing it.

1. *Do you consider yourself a creative person? If yes, why? If not, why not?*
2. *Are there any creative pursuits you did as a child but haven't done for years? If so, what are they?*
3. *Are there some creative or artistic pursuits you would be interested in exploring?/trying out?*
4. *Commit to either starting to integrate a childhood "passion" into your life or choose a new one such as "learning to play the piano" that perhaps you always*

wanted to do as a child but never had the opportunity to do. Identify the next steps for taking action to integrate a new or "old" creative or artistic pursuit into your life. It's helpful to use a two-column table with "activity" heading one column and "timeline" the other.

5. *Support is important to many of us when starting something new and continuing with it. Enlist the support of a friend, colleague or family member to encourage and support you in your new endeavor or invite them to join you in doing it.*

How do we sustain the practice of integrating creative/artistic pursuits into our lives?

1. *After you have engaged in a creative/artistic pursuit, go into your body and note how you feel. Does your body feel lighter? Do you have more energy? Is your mind quieter?*

2. *When you engage in a creative/artistic pursuit over time what changes if any do you notice in your body? Mind? Emotions? Relations? Life in general?*

3. *If you have been engaging in a creative/artistic pursuit with a friend, colleague or family member, what changes, if any, do you notice in them?*

Conclusion

We've learned about the importance of whole-brain thinking and of play and laughter; the links between the arts, health and healing, and some strategies for tapping into our creative side. I would like to close with some words of wisdom from SARK on how to be an artist.

Stay loose. Learn to watch snails. Plant impossible gardens. Invite someone dangerous to tea. Make little signs that say Yes! *and post them all over your house. Make friends with freedom and uncertainty. Look forward to dreams. Cry during movies. Swing as high as you can on a swingset, by moonlight. Cultivate moods. Refuse to "Be responsible." Do it for love. Take lots of naps. Give money away....Believe in magic. Laugh a lot. Celebrate every gorgeous moment. Have wild imaginings, transformative dreams and perfect calm....Giggle with children....Be free....Drive away fear. Play with everything. Entertain your inner child....Build a fort with blankets. Get wet. Hug trees. Write love letters.*

A Creative Companion – How to Free Your
Creative Spirit, 2004

I encourage you to try out the various tools and strategies over the next couple of weeks and notice the ones that resonate with you.

CHAPTER 6

Key #3 - Consciously Create Right and Left Brain/Body Balance

What's all this talk about balance and why is it so important anyway?

We have a lot to learn about balance from Eastern cultures. When we're spinning out of control and stuck on the treadmill and unable to get off, we often intuitively know that we need to create some more balance in our lives. We also may be unsure about how to do that. Included here are some exercises to help you create your own vision of work/life balance, as well as some tools and strategies for creating balance throughout your life. I will also touch on the concepts of feminine and masculine energies and talk about how they influence your body, mind, and the ways you interact with the world beyond yourself.

Traditional concepts of balance

I particularly like the metaphor Austin Vickers shares in his book *Stepping Up To a Life of Vision, Passion and Authentic Power* (2005). He likens balance to a three-legged stool. Vickers refers to the three stool legs as "body, mind, and spirit" and notes "all three of these legs of life are necessary to make us stable and balanced." He cautions that if you are missing one leg of your stool "all of your energy is spent trying to maintain balance and not fall over. You cannot relax. But upon a balanced stool, one can relax, read, work or use it as a tool to do other things."

The cultures of China and India have recognized the importance of a balanced life for more than 2,000 years. Their theories of health and illness are based on the presence (or not) of balance. Traditional Chinese Medicine (TCM) also believes that disease is caused by energy blockage in the body. In order to stay healthy, it is important to keep energy moving throughout our bodies; for example, by regularly practicing *qigong* or *tai chi*, or having therapeutic massages by an experienced practitioner or energy healer.

Feminine and masculine energy

Much has been written about feminine (yin) and masculine (yang) energy. Each person possesses both masculine and feminine energies, but usually one type of energy is more developed/dominant. The dominant energy affects how you perceive yourself, others, and your environments, and how you interact with the world.

The qualities of each type of energy are outlined in the table below.

Feminine Energy (Yin) BEING & GIVING	Masculine Energy (Yang) DOING & RECEIVING
• Creative	• Linear and Logical
• Intuitive	• Analytical
• Collaborative	• Competitive
• Receptive	• Assertive
• Emotional	• Rational
• Passionate	• Determined
• Empathetic	• Objective
• Allow for "flow"	• Goal-directed

As a High Achieving Woman, when you are living life like a spinning top or caught on the treadmill, you are exhibiting many of the characteristics of masculine energy. It is important to be aware of the characteristics of the two energies, as being out of balance has negative impacts on our bodies, minds, relationships, and success at home and work. For example, if we are constantly in our masculine energy, over time it leads to illness, unhappiness, lack of fulfillment, and restlessness. Conversely, if we are dominated by our feminine energy we become resentful, ill, needy, and insecure.

It is important to note that a balance between the yin and yang does not necessarily mean 50% yin and 50% yang. It means "learning to optimize your own unique mix so that your happiness is maximized and your success enhanced." (http://www.themichaelteaching.com/michael/applied-michael/masculine-feminine-duality/)

How can you find and create your unique balance between your masculine and feminine energies? Here are a few suggestions.

1. *Sit down. Close your eyes. Take several deep breaths in through your nose and out through your mouth. Get centered and grounded.*

2. *Reflect on your day. Become an outside observer. Which characteristics of the two energies did you display today, and in which situations?*

3. *Ask yourself if you are living your life more in the masculine than the feminine side or vice versa, and if this is out of balance.*

4. *Ask yourself if you are willing to experiment, to make some changes in your behaviors and notice the impact they have on your body, life, relationships, and creativity at home and at work.*

5. *If the answer is yes, make a conscious decision to change one thing and try it out for a week. It could be the way you relate to your team. Think about this each morning before you get out of bed and make the commitment to yourself. For example, you might say, "I choose today to demonstrate empathy and be receptive to others' ideas; to really listen instead of being in control, assertive, and competitive."*

6. *During the day, start to notice when you become*

"adrenalized"; when you become extremely "geared up" and have trouble sitting still. Take several deep breaths, go inside and ask yourself what it is that is making you feel so anxious. Listen to what comes up for you.

7. *Draw on the other keys to Creative Living and particularly the exercises related to tapping into and expressing your creative side and finding inner peace.*

Work/life balance

Work/life balance is an elusive and personal concept. Elusive, because so many people talk about and strive for it, yet few are able to attain and/or maintain it. Personal, because what work/life balance looks and feels like for you is different from what work/life balance looks and feels like for me.

⌂ *When you think about work/life balance, what thoughts and feelings come up for you? Take a few moments to jot these down.*

Take a few moments to relax. Take several deep breaths and get comfortable. Then think about your personal vision of work/life balance. Answer the following questions.

What does work/life balance look and feel like for you? You may find it helpful to use the stems *I see…* and *I feel….* For example: *I see time in my schedule to have lunch with good friends regularly. I see doing yoga classes four times per week and really being present during these classes. I feel inner calm. I feel there is enough time to do what I want to do each day.*

> **Work/life balance is an elusive and personal concept.**

2. What does your life look and feel like when you are out of balance?

3. What challenges do you face in achieving work/life balance?

4. How committed are you (on a scale of 1 to 10 with 1 being "not at all" and 10 being "100%") to consciously creating your personal vision of work/life balance?

Workaholism: An example of what happens when we're out of balance

Many High Achieving Women become workaholics at some time in their lives. Workaholism is an addiction. It has characteristics in common with other/all addictions: it helps us to cope, numbs us out, and allows us to avoid dealing with deeply held emotions, beliefs, and situations that no longer serve us.

I will use an example from my own life. I can remember believing from a very young age that it was important to "achieve." What achieving meant to me was attaining tangible and measurable results: being the top of my class, winning races, and getting high marks. That focus on achievement and on *doing* carried through into my adult life.

> *Many High Achieving Women become workaholics at some time in their lives. Workaholism is an addiction.*

I remember a time when my daughter, Sara, was just two years old and I was pregnant with my second child. I had federal funding for a project with five people working for me. My son was due to be born part-way through the project. I had maternity leave from my university teaching position, but was not able to lay off my project personnel for three months while I took maternity leave. My husband was working on the other side of the world and though I had a nanny during the day, as soon as I arrived home from work, she left the house.

I recall going to bed thinking about work, awakening with work on my mind, and putting in full days running my project. My mind and body were constantly in motion. I still did aerobics classes and swam throughout my pregnancy, as that was part of my regular routine.

I went into labor while I was at the project office. I finished a day's work and went home, got the house ready and told my nanny I was in labor. My husband wasn't yet home; he was "in flight" and not due home for about 24 hours (our son hadn't been expected for a few more days). I ended up communicating with a colleague who was in labor herself at the nearby Grace Hospital. Her husband was with her and when her labor slowed down she sent him over to accompany me to the hospital. I walked to the hospital with my friend's husband, stopping frequently along the way to breathe through contractions. You can imagine the scene. My membranes ruptured as we entered the emergency room.

I am happy to report that one of my girlfriends, who is a midwife, came to coach me through the birth and I had a healthy baby boy. My husband arrived home the next morning and rushed to the hospital to see his new son, David.

As I had one more class in my program to finish and still had employees, I took only two weeks off after the birth, then went back to work 20 plus hours a week. When David was five weeks old I facilitated a workshop, while my sister sat at the back of the room with my son so that I could nurse him during breaks.

Reflecting on this time in my life I realize I was a *crazy* woman. I never thought that I could or should do anything differently and I managed to accomplish "more than the average bear" in a day. Yet at what cost?

Does any of this sound familiar to you? Though the details of your story will differ, I'm sure it has many elements in common with mine.

It was not until a number of years later that I began to think about balance. I started to incorporate tools and strategies into my life that allowed me the time and space to relax, slow down and "smell the roses." I believe it was my mother's death of metastases from breast cancer that prompted me to examine my life and commit to making positive changes. I am now less driven by the need for external achievement; I allow my core values and my body's wisdom to guide me. It took some time and effort but I do know it is possible to achieve. I can now more consciously choose activities that serve me best.

Tools and strategies for creating work/life balance

In the words of Austin Vickers:

Balance requires us to care for our physical bodies like we care for our houses, our gardens and our cars. To make time in our lives to focus on our minds, stimulating it (them) with nourishing and positive input. And last, but certainly not least, to become aware of and nourish our spirits....To be happy and balanced, our souls must be fed and fueled....Balance in our lives is not a function of genetics or good fortune. It is a carefully and purposefully created habit. Effort should be given each day to work on mind, body and spirit until doing so becomes second nature to us. Having a sturdy, balanced foundation upon which to center our lives allows us to channel the energy and focus that was previously spent trying not to fall [off our stools] toward other more productive and enriching facets of our lives. In other words, having a life of balance means having a life that is not just trying to survive, but having one that is able to thrive.

Stepping Up To a Life of Vision, Passion and Authentic Power, 2005

There are a number of proven tools and strategies to support you as you consciously create balance in your life. A few are included below. The reason I use the phrase "consciously create" is that I believe we all have a choice to envision and create the lives we yearn for.

Ayurveda: creating balance in body, mind and spirit

The science of Ayurveda originated in India more than 5,000 years ago.

The two main guiding principles of Ayurveda are: 1) the mind and body are inextricably connected, and 2) nothing has more power to heal and transform the body than the mind. Freedom from illness depends upon expanding our own awareness, bringing it into balance, and then extending that balance to the body.

http://www.chopra.com/ccl/the-key-to-perfect-health-know-your-ayurvedic-mind-body-type

Ayurveda is based on the belief that our bodies are composed of five essential elements: ether, air, fire, water, and earth. Ayurveda also believes that maintaining balance among these elements is essential for our physical, mental, and spiritual health.

According to Ayurveda, we are all born with three *doshas*, or mind-body types. Most of us have one or two prominent *doshas*. A few of us exhibit all three. Each *dosha* is associated with one of the five essential elements and each *dosha* is associated with certain personality and physical characteristics (Sondhi). To learn more, visit http://www.chopra.com/ccl/what-is-ayurveda, and http://www.chopra.com/ccl/the-key-to-perfect-health-know-your-ayurvedic-mind-body-type

I encourage you to do the *dosha* quiz at http://doshaquiz.chopra.com to identify your unique mind-body type.

Proven Tools and Strategies

1. Identify your unique dosha/mind-body type; learn how to recognize when you're out of balance and what types of food, exercise and lifestyle will assist you to stay in balance.

2. Eat a healthy diet rich in fresh, unprocessed and colorful foods that ideally includes all six Ayurvedic tastes (sweet, salty, sour, pungent, bitter, and astringent) at each meal. Sondhi's book, *The Tastes of Ayurveda,* includes a number of delicious recipes classified according to the *doshas.*

3. Meditate regularly, ideally daily.

4. Practice yoga at least three times a week. A type of yoga I have found particularly helpful in releasing

blocked energy and balancing the right and left sides of my body is yin yoga. It is a meditative form of yoga that is done in a warm room and focuses on holding poses for up to five minutes. This "untangles" our connective tissue, which grows "fuzz" during the night. If we don't stretch and untangle our connective tissue or melt our fuzz, it results in reduced movement and flexibility and ultimately in contractures. Check out Dr. Fuzz on YouTube for more information: http://www.youtube.com/watch?v=VCfclmGrjMk.

5. Get at least six to eight hours of restful sleep each night and go to sleep at a regular hour as much as possible. Sleep is necessary to rejuvenate and repair/heal the body.

6. Spend time in nature every week. When you are feeling particularly stressed, often a 20 to 30 minute walk can relax your mind and enable you to return to work re-energized and with increased focus and creativity.

7. Unplug from technology for at least one entire day each week.

Conclusion

In this chapter we've examined the concept of balance. You've been exposed to Austin Vickers' metaphor of the three-legged stool. You've learned a bit about masculine and feminine energy and explored which energy is most dominant in your life and the impact it has. You've had the opportunity to create your initial personal vision of work/life balance, and learned some strategies for moving toward more balance in your life and work.

I encourage you to review the personal vision of work/life balance you drafted or to take time to create one if you haven't. Read it over and ensure that it is what you truly want your life to look and feel like. Make any adjustments.

I invite you to integrate at least one tool or strategy into your life every day for 21 days (as it takes about three weeks to form a habit). Notice how you feel when you engage in this activity.

Enlist a friend, family member or a coach to support you as you integrate these new behaviors. It is important when making any life changes to have the knowledge of why they're important, the skills or tools to integrate them, and the support to do them. ENJOY!

CHAPTER 7

Key #4 – Live in Alignment with Your Core Values

When I first launched my coaching practice that initially focused on supporting women through various life transitions, I attracted a number of women with various physical ailments from lack of sensation to pain in different parts of their bodies. When I took them through an exercise to help them to clarify their top five core values, an interesting thing happened; for almost all of them a "light bulb" went on. They realized they were in a job or a relationship that was severely out of alignment with one or most of their top five core values.

So what are values and why are they important?

Values are the beliefs and principles that are at the core of our being. We learn them from our parents, from people who have had a significant impact on our lives, and from our life experiences. They "determine" our perceptions of and reactions to people, situations, and events in our lives.

Personal values

Personal values might include achievement, commitment, contribution, connection, integrity, or family. If you are a High Achieving Woman, it is important that you set goals and achieve them on a regular basis in order for you to feel good about yourself. If "contribution" is one of your core values, feeling that you are contributing and making a difference in the world positively affects your well-being.

Have you ever met someone and after having a short conversation with them felt uncomfortable? When someone steps on or pushes up against one of your core values, you may feel uncomfortable, or angry, or protective of another. For example, if "social justice" is important to you, when you see someone behaving disrespectfully to an individual from another cultural group, something fires inside you and you naturally want to stand up for the individual. Getting clear on your personal values helps you better understand yourself and your reactions to others.

> *Getting clear on your personal values helps you better understand yourself and your reactions to others. Knowing your top five core values also assists with your life choices.*

Knowing your top five core values also assists with your life choices. If you choose a business partner who is all about competition and you value collaboration, over time this will bother you. If you value connection and are not able to openly communicate about feelings with a friend or partner, over time the relationship won't grow stronger as you will feel something is missing or that you need more.

Take a few moments to answer the following questions (adapted from work of Sharon Pira).

If you were an animal, what animal would you be? Why would this animal be interesting to you? List the traits you admire in this animal.

2. *What is your favorite film or novel, and why?*

3. *Fill in the blanks in the following two statements with three words each.*

   If _____ were missing in my life, I would be totally miserable.

   When I have _____ I feel peace and harmony with myself and with the world around me.

4. *Notice the values that keep showing up and make a list of the words that showed up more than once. Other possible core values include freedom, financial independence, and health .*

5. *Out of that list, decide on your top five values.*

6. *Define in a short sentence what each of these top five values on your list means to you.*

7. *Write these words on Post-it Notes and put them where you can see them daily.*

8. *Every day for three weeks (remember it takes 21 days to change a habit) review your top five values and rate yourself on a scale of 1 to 10 (10 being "very well" and 1 being "not at all") as to how well you are living those values right now.*

Organizational values

From an organizational or business perspective, values are the standards or principles that guide an organization and describe what it stands for.

Organizational values are wide-ranging and may include collaboration, innovation, teamwork, and excellence. Organizations that are truly "walking their talk" integrate their values in everything they do, from the type of people they hire, to how they reward employees. For example, an organization that values teamwork will hire people who have a track record of being good team players or of building strong high-performing teams. They also reward their employees for being good team players rather than excelling as individuals.

Why is it important to be aware of our own values as well as those of an organization we are working in or thinking about working for?

What happens if we work in an organization that is not compatible with our values?

Can you think of a time when you were working in an organization that wasn't compatible with your values? What was that experience like for you? How did you feel going to work everyday? What did you learn from the experience?

Working in an organization that is out of alignment with our core values leads to stress, anger, and frustration, and over time can cause health issues.

Getting clear on your values and then using that understanding to find or create the work/workplace of

> *Using your core values to assist you in choosing a partner, career, or, workplace is essential to creating a life of health, happiness, true fulfillment, and, inner peace.*

your dreams is possible. Some High Achieving Women try out a number of different jobs early in their careers and leave each one after they feel they've learned all they can from that particular position or environment. Others choose to stay in an organization, move quickly into leadership positions, and become change agents, trying to initiate change within their organizations. Still others realize early in life (or in some cases, later ☺) that they are not meant to work for anyone else. They then create their own organizations (businesses, foundations, not-for-profits).

Conclusion

Identifying your top five core values is critical to better understanding yourself, and your reactions to certain individuals and situations. Using your core values to assist you in choosing a partner, career, or workplace is essential to creating a life of health, happiness, true fulfillment and inner peace.

CHAPTER 8

Key #5 – Believe that You Are Here to Make a Difference

Many High Achieving Women know "in their bones" from a young age that they are here to make a significant difference in the world. They may have no clue as to what that difference is, but they know they are on earth for an important reason.

> When you find your passion and live your life aligned with it, you feel truly joyful, fulfilled and at peace. It lights your fire and fuels your enthusiasm for life.

In order to truly understand yourself and discover what difference you are here to make, it is important to uncover your unique gifts and talents, as well as identify your passions and life purpose.

Discovering passion

I particularly like the definition that Janet and Chris Attwood give to the word "passion" in their book *The Passion Test*. They say that "your passions are the loves of your life…things that are most deeply important to you…things that, when you're doing them or talking about them, light you up." They also note that "passion and love are inextricably intertwined because both arise from the heart. When you follow your passion, you will love your life."

When you find your passion and live your life aligned with it, you feel truly joyful, fulfilled, and at peace. It lights your fire and fuels your enthusiasm for life. You feel that you are indeed doing something that makes a difference in the world and you feel alive.

Sir Ken Robinson, in his book *The Element,* notes that "finding your Element (Passion) is essential to your well-being and ultimate success.…If we find our Element, we all have the potential for much higher achievement and fulfillment." Robinson defines Element as "the meeting point between natural aptitude and personal passion…when people are in their Element they connect with something fundamental to their sense of identity, purpose and well-being. Being there provides a sense of self-revelation, of defining who they really are and what they're really meant to be doing with their lives."

We all have unique strengths and talents to share with the world. Let's take a moment to do a short exercise.

Draw a chart with two columns. In the first column, write down all the things that you are good at, or things that come easily and naturally to you. They could be things such as athletics, mathematics, writing, whatever you feel fits.

2. *In the second column, write down the things you enjoy doing. They could include being in nature, teaching others, using your body, playing piano....If you feel challenged by this, think back to what you enjoyed doing as a child.*

3. *Now look at both lists and circle the items that are similar or identical. Then review the circled items. Go inside and get in touch with the feeling each one evokes inside you. Does it excite you? Does it have little or no effect on you? Rate each item on a scale from 1 to 10 according to the level of passion you have around it*

(1 being "no interest at all" and 10 being "red hot"). I encourage you to finish this exercise. Sharing your findings with others has additional impact as you may gain insights and support from them.

I'd like to emphasize that just being good at something doesn't mean it is our passion or will fulfill us if we work in that area. I'm sure you know someone who was good at math, went on to study mathematics, taught it at school or university and over time was miserable and not at all happy teaching math every day. So what we're good at can provide clues to our passions but are not necessarily connected with them. Things we enjoy doing are normally better clues to what may be our passions. A passion is often a blend of what we love and what we're good at. As well, a passion may change during our lifetime.

What holds you back?

I've categorized the constraints that hold us back from discovering and living our passions as either self-imposed or environmental/external.

Self-imposed constraints include our beliefs and our fears. We may believe that we are not capable or good enough: "I could never do that." We may be afraid of failure, or success, or change: "If I become really successful, I will never have time to myself or to spend with people I care about"

💭 *Think about a belief that may be holding you back and listen to what comes up for you. Think about a fear that may be keeping you from moving forward. Is there a fear that is preventing you from changing careers?*

Another self-imposed constraint is keeping ourselves so busy doing things that we never have time to sit still and reflect on our lives. No time to reflect, no time to experiment or change.

External or environmental constraints include childhood conditioning, family expectations, societal expectations, and life experience. An elementary school teacher may have told us, "You'll never amount to anything." Our parents may have said, "The eldest in our family for the past three generations has been a doctor and so for sure you're going to be one." An example of a societal expectation is the pressure to attain a certain lifestyle (so we can't make a "decent" living being an artist, a musician, and so on). And our life experience may color our perspective of a certain type of work if we've tried a job working for one company in a field we thought we would enjoy and had a tough time with the boss. In reality, it wasn't the work that left a negative impression but rather the personality of the individual who ran the company or was our boss. If we've been in an environment where our fellow employees have been extremely competitive and cutthroat, that too may have colored our perspective on a particular type of work.

📖 *Reflect on your life to date. Can you identify any external or environmental constraints that may be holding you back from discovering and living your passions?*

Life purpose

As we go through life, we often receive glimpses of or clues to our life purpose. Then, like pieces of a puzzle, the clues all come together in an *aha* moment and our life purpose becomes clear.

> We get clues to our life purpose from our top five core values and our strengths.

Much has been written about the importance of finding our purpose. As Marcia Wieder, author of *Making Your Dreams Come True,* says, "The broader you state your purpose the better, because the broader your purpose the more room there is for passion and possibility." Your purpose "touches your heart" and "gets you excited."

Some examples of life purposes might be

- To live life as an adventure and to make a difference in the world
- To inspire and support others to live the best life possible
- To learn and to contribute to making the world a better place

We get clues to our life purpose from our top five core values and our strengths. For example, if one of our strengths (what we're good at) is "connecting with and motivating others," and if we identified "contributing and making a difference in the world" as one of our values, these will guide us as we develop our life purpose statement.

How I found my life purpose

From about the age of three years, I have known I was here make some significant difference in the world. From a young age I had a fascination with different cultures and countries. I knew I wanted to travel the world and explore and understand the various beliefs and practices of the people and cultures I visited. This thread of travel and culture has run through my life. As part of my Masters degree, I studied medical anthropology and sociology. My dissertation involved cultural beliefs and practices surrounding health and illness. When I taught university, I taught physicians and nurses the importance of health beliefs and practices surrounding pregnancy, childbearing, illness and death and how to work more effectively with immigrant clients and their families by taking culture into consideration.

Since the late 1980s, I've had the opportunity to work on a number of projects in Asia, Africa, Europe, and Latin America.

Throughout my professional life and various careers I have worked with groups. Years ago, while a psychiatric nurse, I was trained in group and family therapy and ran these types of groups. Later on, I was "spotted" by the Research and Development manager of a management consulting company while taking a project management course. He asked where I had learned my facilitation skills. I said I had no formal training in facilitating groups, did it naturally, but did have training and experience with therapeutic groups. Soon after, he introduced me to the two other partners in his consulting group and before long I began working as a facilitator and consultant with them. There I learned a number of processes for designing and facilitating both small and large groups. This included strategic and operational planning and multi-stakeholder consultation processes. Later I became certified as a professional facilitator.

I was introduced to the Canadian Institute for Conflict Resolution by a colleague, did some pro bono work with them and later took their "Third Party Neutral" training in mediation and conflict resolution. I've done work on peacebuilding and had the opportunity to live and work in conflict zones such as Afghanistan, Pakistan, and Colombia.

In 2009, I wrote a broad life purpose. It was to live life to the fullest, have fun, and make a difference in the world. It wasn't until May 22, 2013 that I had an incredible *aha* moment when all of the pieces of my life came together and I understood why I had been guided to my various careers and work experiences. I then realized that my true purpose was to build peace in the world one woman at a time. When a woman finds inner peace herself, she can then build peace in her family, community, workplace, and, ultimately, the world. I knew in my bones this was my life purpose.

This is a BIG vision. One that I certainly cannot accomplish alone. It is aligned with my top five core values: contribution, connection, adventure, freedom, love of learning. It builds on my strengths, which include the ability to connect with people from a variety of backgrounds and cultures; the love of and facility to design curricula and participatory processes to train and coach individuals and groups; and skills in coaching, mentoring, facilitation, meditation, and multi-stakeholder consensus building.

My life purpose fuels my passion, which, according to Maxwell in *Put Your Dream to the Test,* is "the starting point of all achievement." He also regards passion as "an enthusiasm that not only gives you energy and focus in the present, but also gives you the power to keep moving toward the future." My experience is that true fulfillment comes from living one's life purpose and enjoying the journey while doing so.

📖 *Take a few minutes now to draft a life purpose statement using the stem:* My life purpose is to… . *Realize this is just a beginning and you will likely need to return to reflect on it and decide if it really truly is* your *life purpose. A couple of good questions to ask related to your life purpose are:* How do I want to be remembered? *and* What am I most passionate about?

Take some time over the next one to two weeks to review your life purpose. Go inside your body and ask yourself the question: Is this my life purpose? *Explore and journal about what comes up for you.*

If you would like to learn more about life purpose, I recommend you listen to Jean Houston's "Three Keys to Discovering and Learning Your Life's Purpose" at http://evolvingwisdom.com/jeanhouston/yourlifepurpose/free-online-class .

Conclusion

In this chapter, you've learned Key #5 - that you are here to make a difference in the world. You had the opportunity to identify your gifts and passions, and started writing your life purpose statement. As passion and life purpose are two important components of a fulfilling, healthy and happy life, I encourage you to do further "work" on these.

CHAPTER 9

Key #6 – Learn from and Embrace Life Transitions

The River of Life

Life's like a river.

Parts of it calm, tranquil and luminous

With reflections of deeper aspects shimmering

within the shoals.

When I am calm and tranquil too, I can focus inwardly

and truly get in touch

With my heart and soul; with what is truly

important to me.

Such moments, thoughtfully taken, help me to reflect on

myself and my life.

*The small eddies may be likened to times in life when I'm
ruffled by undercurrents
Or things I seem to have little or no control over.
Then come the rapidly flowing parts of the river.
These may be likened to adventurous times when I'm not
sure where I'm going.
Everything seems to be flying by, carrying me somewhere;
I'm not sure where.*

*However, if I believe and trust in myself
and in the Universe,
I will eventually come out into the calm and
gentle part of the river.
Things will be balanced and peaceful once more;
Some time to reflect and be still.*

P. Thompson, September, 2000

As we navigate the river of life, many of us may find that change is stressful and challenging. Whether we can control the change or not, whether the change involves the loss of a job, the end of a relationship, or a health crisis such as burnout or cancer, we all have the choice to either embrace or resist a major life change. We may have a friend or colleague who resists change, who is always in "victim mode," complaining about what their boss did to them or how terrible their kids are. They tend to blame others for a particular situation and refuse to take any part of the responsibility for it themselves. Life is always hard and one big drama. Such people seem to move from one crisis to the next.

We also may know other folks who, despite being thrown many challenges (car accidents, illnesses, deaths of family members or friends), are able to bounce right back and get on with their lives after a crisis.

People in the second category view the world differently from those in the first. They view major life challenges as opportunities to learn and grow.

Which type of person are you?

How can you view life's changes and challenges as opportunities?

The difference between change and transition

William Bridges, in his book *Transitions: Making Sense of Life's Changes* (2004), views change as situational and external, such as moving to a new city or becoming a parent. In contrast, he views transition as psychological or internal. Transition, he emphasizes, is the internal work that helps us to reorient and redefine ourselves and incorporate external changes into our lives.

Research and life experience show that if we don't do the internal transition work, then we often recreate the same patterns in our lives. An example is someone who, after three marriages, realizes that she has married three men who are similar (they may even resemble each another). She has dealt with the same issues in each marriage, never resolving them but rather recreating them and remaining unhappy. So in order to move forward and be happy and fulfilled, we need to take time during each transition to do the work that enables us to grow and change patterns that no longer serve us.

The transition journey

At the *Creative Living* Community (CLC), www.creativelivingcommunity.com, we use the metaphor of life as a journey to describe the experience people go through when faced with a major life change. There are phases and signposts along the way that are common to all life transitions.

William Bridges has identified that all major life transitions consist of three phases. In each phase there are opportunities to learn and grow and key work to be done in order to move forward.

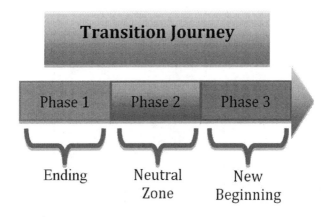

Each phase (ending, neutral zone, beginning) of the journey also has particular "work" associated with it. I will describe each of the three phases and the work it is important for us to do in each one, and will also include tips that will assist you in moving through each phase.

Phase 1 – Ending

An *ending* is the end of a job, relationship, or career. The main work during this phase consists of letting go of the old job, relationship, or career and celebrating the positive aspects and lessons learned from it. So letting go and celebrating are the key points associated with phase 1.

I'd like to share a personal story. In the early 1990s I had a rewarding job at the national level in Canada. I enjoyed my work and the people I worked with. At some point morale started to go down around me. The organization was downsizing and people were reacting to the changing environment in different ways. One of my colleagues, who has since become a dear friend, had a vision to create a new division. It was clearly her passion and in an area where she had a lot of expertise. She mentioned it to her boss who told her to go ahead and put her ideas down on paper, and to include all of the new positions that would be required. Her boss also told her not to bother typing it up but to give it to her in freehand format. My colleague did as she was instructed. She put her heart into designing this new division. When she handed it in, her boss had the work typed up and then presented it to higher-level management for approval as if it was her own idea. To add insult to injury, the boss did not even interview my friend for the position as head of the new division, but instead went outside of the department to bring in someone else.

Serendipitously, around the same time I attended a course given by a man who was the research and development person for a management consulting group. To make a long story short, the course instructor offered me a position in his consulting group, as they needed someone with my background and experience to "open up the health sector" for them. Within six months of attending the course, I left my well-paying and secure job to work for the consulting group without a contract and with a verbal guarantee of eight days of work a month at a fabulous per diem. On leaving my secure job, a number of people asked me why I was leaving such a good job and going to one that was not secure. My response was that I was excited about the new opportunity. I also said that I could no longer work in an organization that wasn't aligned with my values; one that allowed managers to treat people the way my friend had been treated.

So we move on. We leave jobs for particular reasons, and if we are clear why we are leaving one situation and moving into another, then, in my experience, things work out for the better, especially when our actions are aligned with our core values.

Tips for moving through Phase 1 with grace

📖 *Write a letter to the person you are leaving (partner, employer) outlining a number of positive things that you have learned from that particular job or relationship. Then burn the letter ceremoniously. At the same time, feel the positive things about the experience and release any resistance you may have to moving forward.*

📖 *Go back over your life and think about your experiences with endings (the death of a pet, the loss of a loved one, a move or a friend moving away). Reflect on these experiences and notice if there is a pattern in how you deal with endings: Do you avoid saying goodbye? Do you quickly move on and try not to think about the experience or the feelings associated with it? Ask yourself if you are comfortable with the pattern. Has it been serving you well or would you like to change it?*

Take a moment to think about one particular ending or loss you have experienced in your life. Feel it. What did it feel like for you? How has it affected how you have dealt with other endings or losses in your life? Write down your thoughts and feelings.

We all develop our own responses to endings in our lives. We may deal with them abruptly by saying goodbye and moving on quickly, or we may deal with them slowly and gradually. How you have dealt with endings in the past will affect how you work through any future life transition.

The impact of a transition also varies greatly from one person to another. Some people fall apart during a divorce and others take it in stride. If we initiate the major life change, it is usually easier to negotiate than if the change is out of our control or initiated by someone else. If we've just come out of a long-term relationship and the separation or divorce was not initiated by us, it is helpful to reflect on the relationship, both the positive aspects of it and the lessons learned.

We all develop our own responses to endings in our lives. We may deal with them abruptly by saying goodbye and moving on quickly, or we may deal with them slowly and gradually. How you have dealt with endings in the past will affect how you work through any future life transition.

Based on this, writing a letter to your ex-partner and either keeping it or burning it ceremoniously can assist us to move forward. Keeping the lessons learned top of mind can also assist us when we envision the new partner and relationship of our dreams. I will speak more about a visioning process later.

Phase 2 – The Neutral Zone

Are you feeling stuck? Angry? Confused? Uncertain of what to do next? If so, you are likely in the neutral zone (phase 2 of Bridge's model). The main work of the neutral zone is "getting clear." Phase 2 provides the opportunity to envision the job or relationship of your dreams. It is important during this phase to reconnect with yourself and clarify who you are and what is really important to you. It is also important to get clear on your values during this time.

Tips for embracing the neutral zone with grace

1. *Slow down. For example, rather than getting on the Internet and going out dating right away at the end of a relationship, take some time for yourself.*

2. *Reconnect with yourself and what you enjoy. Take some time alone to think about when you felt really happy and alive. Think about things you used to do but haven't done for some time, or things you've dreamed of doing and have never taken the time for. Begin doing them. Choose one activity and notice how you feel when you are engaged in it.*

3. *Get in touch with and acknowledge your feelings, rather than pushing them down and not experiencing them. This begins the process of healing from the inside out.*

4. *Express those feelings through journaling, painting, drawing, dancing, etc.*

5. *Nurture/pamper yourself. Go for a massage, buy a new outfit, have a bubble bath, do something special for yourself. Remember that you are special and deserve the best.*

6. *Spend time in nature. Go for a walk by yourself in a nearby park, or plan a hike with a friend. Being in nature is grounding and helps us clear negative energy, relax, and clear our mind.*

7. *Exercise. Do something physical, be it a good walk, yoga, or a swim. Exercise helps the energy flow and also assists in getting rid of tension, anger, and stress.*

8. *Reach out to a friend, counselor, or life coach for support.*

After working through the uncomfortable feelings associated with the neutral zone, it is important to *get clear* on the new job, relationship, or whatever you want in your life.

📖 *Use the stem* I see...*and write a list of attributes you want (in a new relationship, job, home, etc.).*

I can attest to using this visioning process and getting all the things I wrote down in my visions. One time was when I was getting clear about the relationship and partner of my dreams. I wrote down all the attributes I wanted in a partner, including: height between five foot nine inches and six foot two inches; an amazing communicator; someone who loves the outdoors and being in nature; someone who makes me laugh. I got them all in my new partner. I feel truly blessed by the special relationship Alan and I share. There was a time in my life when I didn't believe such intimacy was possible.

The other time was several years ago when Alan and I decided to move to the area we now live in. In April of that year we sat down with a pad of paper and, being a facilitator, I wrote the stem *I see...* related to the new home Alan and I would purchase there. We took turns contributing our wishes to the list. For example, I wrote, "I see a home with a beautiful view of Lake Okanagan." Alan said, "I see a gym and yoga room with a view of the lake." Then I wrote, "I see a master bedroom with French doors going onto a balcony that overlooks the lake." You guessed it, within a month of creating the list we drove to the area where we wanted to move and went out with a realtor for a few hours. By the next evening, we had purchased the home of our dreams that included every point we had written down in our vision.

I truly believe that if we see any major transition as an opportunity for growth, fun, and self-learning, wonderful things will happen in our lives.

Phase 3 – The New Beginning

The third phase of the transition journey, the new beginning, is when you take action on the vision you created during the time in the neutral zone. This phase can be likened to a butterfly breaking out of its cocoon, and it can be a time of real transformation, particularly if you've taken the time to learn and grow in the neutral zone.

> *If you don't take the time to reflect, learn, and grow in each phase of the transition journey, you may find that you keep re-creating the same patterns in your life.*

Tips for embracing the new beginning phase with grace

📖 *Post the vision you created in a place where you will see it every day. Make a point of looking at it at least once a day (ideally several times a day).*

📖 *Write an affirmation related to your vision such as, "I am doing the job of my dreams — one that is aligned with my values that energizes me and makes me feel alive and fulfilled every day — a job where I support, motivate and inspire others daily." Then post this affirmation in a place where you will see it daily. Read it aloud several times each day and* feel *how you will feel when you reach that goal.*

📖 *Develop an action plan. List key activities and realistic completion dates. Include descriptions of what success will look and feel like when you've completed each key action.*

For those who are auditory learners, you may wish to record your affirmations and your action plan and play them to yourself in your office, car, at home, or when you work out in order to internalize them and make them real in your life.

If you don't take the time to reflect, learn, and grow in each phase of the transition journey, you may find that you keep re-creating the same patterns in your life. If you want a life of happiness, health, balance, and fulfillment, it is helpful to understand the transition journey process and also to do the work to learn and grow in each phase. A life coach can assist you with this process.

CHAPTER 10

Key #7 - Find Inner Peace and Build Peace in Your Family, Community, Workplace…the World

Many High Achieving Women are restless from a young age. We are on a constant quest for knowledge, meaning and experience. We set a goal, achieve it and swiftly move on to the next project (often more than one at a time ☺). We are always in motion and focused on achievement.

Some High Achieving Women may believe that inner peace cannot coexist with their drive to succeed. They worry that if they slow down, take some time to explore and find some inner peace, they will lose their passion and no longer be successful. From experience, I can tell you that finding inner peace allows you to be more successful, happy, content, and fulfilled in all aspects of your life.

When you think about finding inner peace you may visualize yourself on a mountaintop in lotus position, far away from your current reality. Realistically though, as appealing as that image might be, most of us don't have the time or the money to spend our lives meditating on mountaintops. I'd like to share a poem that for me describes inner peace (source unknown).

> *Some High Achieving Women may believe that inner peace cannot coexist with their drive to succeed.*
>
> ....
>
> *From experience, I can tell you that finding inner peace allows you to be more successful, happy, content, and fulfilled in all aspects of your life .*

Peace.
It does not mean to be in a place
where there is no noise, trouble
or hard work.
It means to be in the midst of
these things and still be calm
in your heart.

What does inner peace look and feel like for you? Take a few moments to get quiet and go inside. Ask yourself the question, "What does inner peace look and feel like for me?" Notice what comes up. Write down your feelings and draw or otherwise capture a visual of what you experienced.

For me, inner peace includes:

- Feeling centered and grounded
- Feeling and believing that I am enough
- Feeling that I belong and am safe
- Believing that I am part of something greater than myself and am here to make a difference in the world
- Awakening each day with a smile on my face and a song in my heart
- Being grateful for all that I have
- Believing the Universe is friendly and here to love and support me
- Being okay with uncertainty
- Feeling loved and nurtured when I take time for myself (not feeling guilty)

- Standing in my power, confidently expressing what I believe, and asking for what I want (not worrying about what others think or say)
- Having balance in my life
- Listening to and trusting in my body's wisdom
- Being in touch with and regularly tapping into my creative side
- Knowing what my passions, core values, and life purpose are, and living a life aligned with them.

Finding inner peace

What can you do to find inner peace?

Some proven strategies and powerful practices for finding inner peace include:

- Quieting your busy mind through yoga, meditation, listening to relaxing music
- Engaging in a passion such as dancing, gardening, painting, where you lose track of time and focus on the activity rather than your "to do" list

- Participating in mindfulness practices (such as walking meditation) that enable you to be in the present moment
- Reclaiming and owning all parts of yourself
- Forgiving yourself and others
- Listening to and trusting in your body's wisdom and using it to guide your decisions and actions
- Living a life in alignment with your core values
- Engaging in work you are passionate about
- Being grateful for what you have
- Tapping into and expressing your creative side regularly
- Surrounding yourself with people who nourish you rather than sap your energy
- Spending time regularly in nature

Many of the strategies and practices above have been discussed in detail in previous chapters. Integrating the tools and strategies shared in those chapters will contribute to you finding inner peace. This chapter will focus on those proven practices not discussed elsewhere, such as forgiveness, reclaiming and owning all parts of ourselves, and gratitude.

Forgiveness

Forgiveness is the ultimate source of peace, healing and inner happiness.

Nawang Khechog

Forgiveness heals emotional wounds, which has an impact on our mind, body and spirit. It is as important to forgive ourselves for things we've done in the past that we don't feel good about as it is to forgive others.

David Simon, in his book *Free to Love, Free to Heal,* notes that "we navigate the path to emotional freedom through forgiveness." From his years of experience as a mind-body physician he found that "forgiveness expands our hearts…and every heart has the power to forgive."

Mindfulness and a forgiveness meditation

Mindfulness means maintaining a moment-by-moment awareness of our thoughts, feelings, bodily sensations, and surrounding environment.… Mindfulness also involves acceptance, meaning that we pay attention to our thoughts and feelings without judging them – without believing, for instance that there's a "right" or "wrong" way to think or feel in a given moment. When we practice mindfulness, our thoughts tune into what we're sensing in the present rather than rehashing the past or imagining the future.

Jack Kornfield, *The Wise Heart*

A mindfulness tool that facilitates forgiveness of self and others is the forgiveness meditation. One process for this has been developed by Jack Kornfield, a psychologist trained in Eastern and Western psychology. I encourage you to take ten minutes to listen to his guided forgiveness meditation on YouTube. https://www.youtube.com/watch?v=PbHKCy4f6Dk

Practicing regular forgiveness meditation can assist us in letting go of the negative emotions and beliefs that we carry in our bodies and minds.

Reclaiming and owning all parts of ourselves

I'd like to share a story that illustrates the importance of reclaiming and owning all parts of ourselves.

I came to realize fairly recently that I hadn't owned the fact that I am an entrepreneur. Most of my work has been with public sector organizations in Canada and internationally, so I didn't really feel like I was a "genuine" entrepreneur. For some reason, it never felt quite right to claim that I had my own business. When I sat with that for a while, I realized I've been an entrepreneur since I was quite young. My girlfriend and I caught and sold minnows to fishermen when we were about nine years old. I also made bracelets out of shells and tried to sell them. I had the typical lemonade stand at a young age. Between the ages of nine and thirteen, I had a card and small gifts business. I would go from house to house, show people my catalogue, and ask them for orders. When they asked me what I was saving for, I said I was saving for my trip around the world. Which, by the way, I took when I was 30. ☺

So what made me not want to own up to being an entrepreneur? When I went inside and reflected, I noticed that one of my beliefs was that selling is not positive or acceptable for me. I have recently changed my thinking and beliefs about being an entrepreneur and now see and feel the positive aspects of it. These include: working with clients who are going through similar experiences I have been through and supporting them, speaking from my heart about lessons I have learned on my journey, truly living my passion daily, connecting with other like-minded entrepreneurs, and making a positive difference in the world through my work.

Have you had a similar experience that you'd like to share? How did you "own" that part of yourself? Is there a part of yourself you're not owning? Are you ready to reclaim it/view it in a positive light?

Identifying our negative or limiting beliefs is the first step to being able to release old patterns that are holding us back from achieving our true potential. Owning all of who we are and framing all parts of ourselves in a positive light contribute to our happiness, health, and contentment.

Gratitude

Gratitude is not about "looking at the bright side" or denying the realities of life. Gratitude goes much deeper than that. It's about learning from a situation, taking the good to help deal with other challenges in the future. It's about finding out that you have more power over your life than you previously imagined. You can stop being a victim of your circumstances and reach out to the joy in living. If you open your heart to the good in your life, gratitude becomes as much a part of your life as breathing.

Joan Buchman
http://www.cfidsselfhelp.org/library/the-healing-power-gratitude

There is a growing body of research that points to the health benefits of gratitude; the importance of being and feeling grateful for who we are, what we have, and where we are in our lives.

Robert Emmons and his colleagues at the University of California Davis, in their book *Thanks!: How the Practice of Gratitude Can Make You Happier* (2008), cite a number of studies that demonstrate that those who practice gratitude regularly "reap emotional, physical and interpersonal benefits." Those who regularly kept a gratitude journal reported feeling better about their lives in general, reported fewer illness symptoms, and were more optimistic about the future.

I encourage you to keep a gratitude journal. Write down, either in the morning or at night every day, five things you are grateful for. Another way to remember to be grateful is to have visual clues such as fridge magnets or Post-it Notes in your environment to remind you of your blessings.

Building peace in our family, community, workplace…the world

As High Achieving Women, we have many opportunities to build peace through the behaviors we model in our interactions with others. For example, with our family members, when we are centered, grounded and at peace we truly focus on each individual and connect with them at the heart level. They then feel listened to, understood, accepted, and loved. Likewise in the workplace, if a colleague gets upset or angry we can show empathy and understanding rather than reacting to them with frustration or as if they are a threat.

When at peace, we can "be in the moment" instead of mulling over the past or worrying about the future. When we are positive and optimistic, that energy positively affects the people around us and the environment we are in. This also holds true for the various communities with which we engage, whether they be not-for-profit boards or community associations.

Conclusion

Finding inner peace is not only one of the seven keys to *Creative Living*, it is also an outcome of the "learning to dance with life" process. In order to find inner peace, we need to integrate all of the seven keys to *Creative Living* into our lives, including the proven strategies and powerful practices associated with them.

PART III

Sharing Your Dance with the World

CHAPTER 11

Getting Involved in the
Creative Living Community

I've enjoyed sharing the process of "learning to dance with life" with you. I hope you have experienced positive changes in your life as a result of integrating the seven keys to *Creative Living* into it. I hope that you are now taking time to nurture and celebrate yourself, and that you are making conscious choices that enable you to live a life *you* love.

Creative Living is indeed a journey; it doesn't happen in three months or even a year. We are constantly learning and growing. Continuing to integrate the proven strategies and powerful practices will enable you to learn life's lessons with increasing ease and grace, and to experience enhanced clarity, creativity, health, fulfillment and inner peace.

A fun way to support yourself while you dance with life is to identify a dance you love either doing or watching. If you're an artist, feel free to draw yourself dancing. You may prefer to cut a picture out of a magazine or find one online and post it where you consciously see it every day. May it represent your new life and how *you* dance with it. You may also have a song that you love the lyrics to. I encourage you to integrate that into your days as well; it will also support you on your unique journey.

Creative Living is about being flexible, living without fear, greeting each day as an opportunity to share your gifts and connect with yourself and with others from a place of understanding, love, and compassion. It includes spending more time in your right brain so you can live life to the fullest and be the best you can be using your talents

> *This book lays the foundation for the Creative Living Facilitator Program, a program that will train and license women to share the seven keys to Creative Living with groups of other women around the world.*

to create peace, joy, and fulfillment in your life and in the lives of those you touch. It's knowing you're on this planet for a reason, and contributing your gifts to make the world a place of love, joy, peace, and harmony.

Creative Living includes viewing each life transition and challenge as an opportunity for learning and growth and then embracing that change. It involves believing that the Universe/Higher Power/God (whatever you choose to call the Source) supports you and provides you with what you need.

The Creative Living *Facilitator Program*

This book lays the foundation for the *Creative Living* Facilitator Program, a program that will train and license women to share the seven keys to *Creative Living* with groups of other women around the world. To learn more, contact pam@creativelivingcommunity. com and put *Creative Living* Facilitator Program in the subject line.

The Creative Living *Community and how you can get involved*

It is my hope that everyone who reads this book will be inspired to participate in the *Creative Living* Community in some way. There are various ways to get involved.

1. Post your comments, *aha* moments, and experiences related to reading the book on our Facebook page at https://www.facebook.com/CreativeLivingCommunity. I'd love to hear from you and how using the seven keys is affecting your life.

2. Sign up for my blog "Confessions of a High Achieving Woman" at http://creative-livingcommunity.com/blog/ and share your comments whenever it feels right.

3. If you think that additional support in the form of individual or group coaching might be help-

> *Know that we are all interconnected. Just as throwing a pebble into a pond causes ripples to extend out from the center, living a life that integrates the keys to Creative Living contributes to making the world a better place.*

ful for you, visit http://creativelivingcommunity. com/coaching/ to learn more about *Creative Living* Coaching programs or email pam@creative-livingcommunity.com.

4. If you wish to become licensed as a *Creative Living* Facilitator and share the seven keys with groups of women and contribute to building peace in the world one woman at a time, contact support@ creativelivingcommunity.com to learn more about the training process.

5. To enquire about having me speak to your group or organization, visit http://creativelivingcommunity. com/speaking/.

As you continue your journey

Continue to integrate the seven keys into your life and reap the benefits. From your new patterns of being more responsive and less reactive, living a life in alignment with your core values, using your body as well as your brain to make decisions, being more grounded, you will notice the positive influence you have on those around you and how much more you enjoy life.

Know that we are all interconnected. Just as throwing a pebble into a pond causes ripples to extend out from the center, living a life that integrates the keys to *Creative Living* contributes to making the world a better place.

My vision of what the Creative Living *Community movement can achieve*

I see a world free of war and violence;

One where all cultures and religions are accepted;

Where all people are respected and treated with respect;

Where people live together in communities that model the values of contribution, collaboration, caring and connection;

Where people are truly connected with who they are and the gifts they have to share;

Where creativity is valued and everyone knows how to tap into and express their creative side;

Where people have the courage to reach out for support when they need it.

I see a world where people trust their bodies, value their own wisdom, and know when and how to say no;

One that believes in the power of groups and synergy, that the whole is greater than the sum of the parts;

A world where women and men stand together as partners.

What is your vision? Would you like to join us and actively engage in building peace in the world one woman at a time?

About the Author

Pamela Thompson loves to travel and connect with people from a variety of backgrounds and cultures. She has had the opportunity to live and work in such countries as Afghanistan, Colombia, Pakistan, Nigeria, and Russia. She believes that *life is an adventure to be lived to the fullest* and is on a global mission *to build peace in the world one woman at a time.*

Pam loves the outdoors and being in, on, and by the water. She lives with her partner, Alan, in the beautiful Okanagan Valley and has two grown children she is so proud of.

Through her fun and highly participatory keynotes, workshops, and group and one-on-one coaching programs, Pam supports busy women to transform their lives from constantly *doing* and *giving* into healthy, balanced lives THEY design and love.

Pam brings to her coaching a diverse background as a nurse, academic, professional facilitator, project manager and consultant in North America, Europe, and the developing world. She was commissioned by the Pan American Health Organization (PAHO) to research and write "Health Promotion: Improving the Health Status of Women and Promoting Equity" (1993) and is an honored fellow of the Canadian Institute for Conflict Resolution.

Pam has created two successful management consulting businesses since the early 1990s and is currently President of Global Village Consulting, in addition to Creative Life Coaching. She is Founder of the *Creative Living* Community and invites you to join the community at www.creativelivingcommunity.com and to connect with her on Facebook https://www.facebook.com/CreativeLivingCommunity.

Made in the USA
Charleston, SC
13 October 2015